The SE Switch: Evolution and Our Self-Esteem

The SE Switch: Evolution and Our Self-Esteem

by

Leonard A. Zimmerman, M.D.

RIVERCROSS PUBLISHING, INC.
Orlando

ISBN: 1-58141-021-2

Library of Congress Catalog Card Number: 00-036914

First Printing

Library of Congress Cataloging-in-Publication Data

Zimmerman, Leonard A., 1942–
    The SE switch : evolution and our self-esteem / by Leonard A. Zimmerman.
        p. cm.
    Includes bibliographical references.
    ISBN 1-58141-021-2
    1. Self-esteem. 2. Genetic psychology. I. Title: Self esteem switch. II. Title.

    BF697.5.S46 Z56 2000
    155.2—dc21
                                        00-036914

Contents

Preface   vii
Introduction   xi

Chapter 1 Current Notions of SE and The SE Switch 21
Chapter 2 Evolutionary Psychology   31
Chapter 3 The SE Switch   41
Chapter 4 Traditional Views of SE   49
Chapter 5 The SE Switch in Operation   55
Chapter 6 Pride and Prestige   67
Chapter 7 "Being Right"   81
Chapter 8 SE Impairment   95
Chapter 9 Arrogance and Anger   103
Chapter 10 Does it Matter?   109
Post Script   123

Bibliography   125

Preface

When I first wondered if evolution played some role in why humans experienced certain feelings, or behaved in certain ways, I had no idea what kind of literature existed on the subject. The first book I encountered was "On Human Nature," by Edward O. Wilson, Professor of Entomology at Harvard. His lucid writing created an excitement and sense of adventure which led me to pursue further reading in this field, something I have been doing now for more than ten years. As I learned more about Evolutionary Psychology, or Sociobiology, I felt something brewing, which made me think I might be able to make some contribution to the field. At first, I did not know what form that would take, and certainly not what the topic would be.

Being a lifelong athlete, I sometimes marveled at the range of emotions I experienced during competition. As some of my ideas about evolution and human behavior began to take shape, I also took notice of some of my friends' reactions to their performance during competition in tennis, and later golf. I began to compare notes with them about what emotions they were aware of during and after participation in these sports. In golf, particularly, there was both evidence of dejection and sometimes despair when one's performance went poorly. When specifically questioned about how they felt at these times, the responses confirmed the apparent unpleasant states of mind. Since the people I observed and talked to were highly educated, well adjusted individuals, who also had long prior histories of athletic competition, I wondered what the genesis of some of these feelings might be. It seemed the explanation might lie beyond the usual psychological and psychiatric notions related to how we respond to success and failure, and it occurred to me that what we felt might not be related to life experiences or upbringing, but rather to some hard-wired evolutionary mechanism within us. As I explored this idea, I realized that not only might this be the case, but there probably were many other areas of everyday life which might be affected by such a phenomenon.

The idea I present in this book is the product of my own lifelong curiosity and interest in biology and, more recently, in evolution. This idea has also taken its roots from the thinking of many fine scientists who have published scholarly articles and books, describing hard evidence for some of the aspects of our human nature. I have been particularly affected by the works of Edward O. Wilson, Matt Ridley, Daniel Goleman, and Richard Dawkins. The bibliography lists all of the references which are most pertinent to the concepts discussed in this book.

My patients, having been some of my best teachers, provided the milieu for further study, and the discipline of medicine instilled within me the principles enabling me to think more about human behavior. While I am not a formal expert in evolution, psychiatry, psychology, anthropology, or philosophy, the experience of many years of medical practice encouraged me to become more intimate with those fields. Treating patients brought me face to face with the full gamut of human dilemmas and their attendant emotions. The challenge to better understand what kinds of forces caused patients, with and without illness, to feel and behave the way they do, stimulated me to look further into those disciplines than I had during my formal education.

The investigative journey I embarked upon, to better understand those emotions and behaviors relating to self-esteem, is what eventually led me to formulate the new idea presented in this book. The proposed model of the SE Switch was born of intuitive and inferential aspects of my mind and its name chosen apropos a device capable of generating powerful feelings in response to rapidly changing life circumstances.

Introduction

"A man cannot be comfortable without his own
approval"

Mark Twain, 1906

This book is about self-esteem. It is an attempt to look at a
concept with which we are all familiar and to try to see
that concept with some new understanding. As with many
things which appear simple on the surface and universally
understood in everyday conversation, the task can become
difficult when one tries to define them. Feelings of love,
loneliness, anger, and happiness are examples of these
kinds of things. Everyone knows what is meant when you
talk about them, but in trying to sort out their essential
nature, even the philosophers are hard pressed to agree, or
even to find the words which best define them. Perhaps
some are like the primary colors, easily known but not de-
finable other than to call them primary.

The concept of self-esteem falls into this category of
apparent simplicity. Most people understand immediately
what is meant when the term is used. It is also not difficult
at first blush to define the meaning of this term. But when
looked at deeply, the appropriate definition may derive
from more complex origins than we had imagined and,
unlike the primary colors, may be understandable by thinking and description.

It is the thesis of this book that, *there is a new way to*
view the concept of self-esteem; namely that it is an evolutionary

mechanism within us embodied in a device I call The Self-Esteem Switch. The role self-esteem plays in our everyday lives is much more prevalent and pervasive than we think. It is my belief this mechanism is operational in all of us to some extent all the time and that the effects of its operation affect much of what we do everyday.

By understanding the origins and nature of this evolutionary equipment, it may help us to see some things in our lives from a new perspective. We may even learn how to react differently and more sensibly to certain events which occur as our lives unfold.

The main concept presented in this book is my own idea. There is no proof for the model I will propose. To the extent that no laboratory testing of a "switch" relating to self-esteem has been performed, and that my credentials pertain mostly to the field of medicine, I am open to criticism. I take some comfort that the existence of Freud's Id, Ego, and Superego have never been verified or localized to particular parts of the brain.

As a practicing physician, I am keenly aware of the danger of putting forth a theory without good scientific data. I could not recommend a treatment to one of my patients without such information. However, since the ideas I put forth here are not intended to have any immediate medical applicability, I feel comfortable in presenting them in the hope that they may prove interesting to the general reader. If these concepts also provoke some interest among those in the scientific field, I will be especially pleased.

Several vignettes will now be presented which I hope will set the stage for the rest of the book. Each is brief and some are recognizable as everyday kinds of events. Some are unique, but all have been chosen to provide examples of how self-esteem may tie into some things which, at first glance, might not seem to have much to do with that concept. We will come back to some of these examples as the book unfolds demonstrating how evolution has provided the means within us to allow us to feel certain emotions and also to behave in predictable ways.

The fans pouring into the stadium do not need to wait for the contest to begin. Their excitement and enthusiasm is unbridled and spontaneous, many screaming wildly with cries of joy proclaiming the Miami Dolphins' greatness and predicting their imminent victory over the Buffalo Bills in this playoff game. The individual calls occasionally blend into a chorus of chanting, unchoreographed but marvelously well tuned. The surprising intensity of the sound seems to be taken for granted by the same crowd from which it emanates, their thoughts primarily focused on the excitement to come and the pleasures to be had if the Dolphins can prevail. Inside, as the starting teams are announced, the ferocity of the boos directed at the Bills, and the jubilantly adoring cheers for Miami, rock the stadium. The game begins, and a state of ecstacy instantly envelops the crowd as a Dolphin player intercepts a Buffalo pass. The quality of the sound produced clearly reflects this most sublime pleasure. Moments later this emotion turns into one of equal intensity, but of miserable despair, when the Bills cause the Dolphins to fumble the ball away.

An American born Japanese sumo wrestler has captured the national title of grand sumo wrestling in Japan. American sports writers described the national pride in the U.S., an American born athlete having achieved this mark. Japanese are not sure whether to award him the honor, but reluctantly do so. The emotions involved on each side of the Pacific are confused and reactions restrained. Are the Americans really proud? Have the Japanese people lost or won?

Two male lions are vying for the affections of an available female. They circle, study, and survey each other, then make preliminary gestures of aggression. Roars are exchanged, postures taken and, abruptly, one backs off, defeated without a battle, allowing the other unobstructed access to the lioness.

A beautiful woman preens and grooms herself in front of a mirror preparing for her day's work at the office. Gradually, as she achieves the desired affect, she notices a definite sense of pleasure building within. Finally, the work finished, the pleasure transforms into a sense of well-being and confidence as she is about to begin her day.

A television camera has been installed in a classroom of the predominantly black, Howard University Law School to record the immediate reaction of students to the long awaited announcement of the verdict in the O.J. Simpson criminal trial. There is overwhelming jubilation among the students as the decision is announced, the students standing, gesticulating, and cheering. Among other highly educated people, there is the general belief that an injustice has been done, and there is sadness and quiet.

A disgraced President Nixon resigns from office because of scandal. An intense investigation has exposed conspiracies, lies, hatred, pettiness, vindictiveness, and misuse of power. After he is out of office, he spends the rest of his life trying to rehabilitate his image. Some, who worked in his administration, rationalize their loyalty even after learning of his bigotry.

An elderly, retired lifetime employee of the FBI falls prey to an old scam involving phony detectives who request her assistance to catch a thief at her bank. As instructed, she withdraws a large sum from her bank account, turns it over to them "to be used as bait for the thief," and never sees the money again. As someone who should have known better, she complains to her doctor about "what our society has come to" and how "law enforcement is not doing a very good job." Her doctor, sensing her need not to be critical of herself, commiserates with her about our cruel world.

These examples of human and animal behavior, seemingly unrelated, have as a common feature the manifestations of some of the forces operating around issues of self-esteem. The ecstacy or agony felt by sports fans watching their team, the innate signals which animals experience as instinct guides their behavior, and the sometimes subtle internal messages people intuitively respond to are phenomena relating to the self-evaluative process we call self-esteem. While clearly there are many different kinds of factors at play in the behaviors described in these examples, it is the contention of this book that the emotional forces associated with our own evaluations of self play a much greater role in our everyday lives than we have traditionally thought. *I believe much of what affects and motivates us in our personal lives, as well as in society as a whole, is due to both conscious and unconscious drives produced by the evolutionary mechanism within us I have chosen to call The Self-Esteem Switch. This internal device is what creates the emotions and some of the behavior just described.*

There is a large popular literature regarding self-esteem and how to attain high levels of it; also a large psychologic and psychiatric body of literature, as well as sociologic and classical philosophical opinions about this topic. Most of the material in scholarly works has dealt with those factors that make for good or bad self-esteem and what the consequences of those states of mind may mean for the individual or society. To my knowledge, there is no existing theory as to why and how evolution has created this phenomenon within us we call self-esteem, and why it then plays such a central role in our normal every day human behavior. Internal signals relating to feelings about self-evaluation may guide us in making choices, and may either motivate us to pursue activities which produces feelings that make us feel delighted with ourselves, or may cause us to avoid situations producing feelings that make us very unhappy about ourselves.

In order to understand some of these concepts, it will be necessary to discuss some aspects of science. The field of Sociobiology, an outgrowth of the science of evolution, became a formal discipline in 1976 with publication of the seminal work "Sociobiology," written by Edward O. Wilson. This treatise concerns itself with those aspects of animal and human behavior which are believed to be determined directly by our genetic makeup, the product of millions of years of evolution.

The theory postulates that human behaviors may not just be related to what our parents or grandparents were like, but also may resemble other forms of animals, much less complex in their structural makeup than humans, but sometimes with remarkably similar patterns for individual and group behavior. The theory suggests there are traits or instinctive kinds of characteristics which have become part of human beings through the evolutionary process, and that much of what we call human nature may be the product of this process. The study of primates, our closest genetic relatives, has provided a great fund of information for analyzing similarities between human and "monkey" natures.

As with other great new theories, this one has been met with tremendous controversy in the scientific community. Many seasoned evolutionary scientists believe the theory goes too far in attempting to explain complex parts of our human nature on the basis of our genetic makeup. Even among evolutionists, there is great disagreement about the roots of many aspects of our behavior, credit still being given to cultural and learned sources, rather than to genetic determination.

Because of the anger the term Sociobiology engendered among many scientists, a newer term, Evolutionary

Psychology, has come gradually to replace it. A large volume of work in scientific papers and books already exists in this field and is rapidly proliferating. Lay articles on topics in Evolutionary Psychology now appear regularly in newspapers and periodicals. While the nature versus nurture arguments will continue to rage regarding why we feel and behave the way we do, there is ample evidence to credit genetically determined behavior in us, similar to what we call instinct in animals, as the basis for much of what we consider to be our human nature.

I believe that aspect of our human nature we refer to as self-esteem is one of those conceptualizations deriving from the evolutionary process, and therefore from our genetic origins. Contrary to classical psychological and psychiatric theories, I suggest what we call self-esteem is actually a set of emotional signals, products of built-in devices of our human brains. These devices were developed through many years of evolution and natural selection, and came about because they were aides to the organism's survival, rather than functioning simply as a means to conceptualize ourselves. In other words, humans have built-in mechanisms sending information from one part of the brain to another, designed to help us survive. In the modern world, we often have different stimuli activating these mechanisms. We also may interpret the messages sent by such devices in ways which have little to do with our continued existence, but may indeed have the intensity of feeling as if they did.

Those very powerful feelings related to a sense of good or bad self-esteem may be genetically programmed to aid us in making choices, and thereby increase our chances of survival. Like the male lions who instinctively know which would survive a battle to the death for the female, we are constantly receiving internal signals telling us what to do next. Both the euphoric feeling of high self-esteem and the miserably unpleasant feeling of low self-esteem are not simply emotions that happens to occur in people, but rather well developed signals which our brains produce at an unconscious level and then recognize at a conscious level, encouraging or discouraging certain types of behavior.

In the chapters which follow I will describe what I believe are the most important functions the self-esteem mechanism accomplishes for us, and also how and why it affects us in everyday ways, producing feelings, emotions, and often actions which may shape our lives.

Since the term "self-esteem" will appear many times in the text, I have chosen to abbreviate it with the designation, "SE."

In addition, since there are always a number of explanations which could account for any particular event or behavior, I have relied to some extent on the Occam's Razor logical principle. Sir William Of Occam, a 14th century philosopher said, "One should not increase, beyond what is necessary, the number of entities required to explain anything."

This theory assumes that simpler explanations are inherently better than complicated ones. Many of the issues discussed in this book have the potential of great complexity. In trying to understand the prime mover or root cause of some of them, I have relied on this medieval principle.

The SE Switch:
Evolution and Our
Self-Esteem

Chapter 1

Current Notions of SE and The SE Switch

*"I began to understand that self-esteem isn't every-
thing; it's just that there is nothing without it."*
Gloria Steinem, 1992

Books abound on how to improve SE. Everyone knows
that feeling confident is an important feature of whether
an endeavor is likely to be successful or not. It is easy to
spot a self assured person by noticing the quality of his
facial features, gait, carriage, speech, and other body language. It is also often easy to see lack of confidence in someone by making similar observations. Athletes who feel they
can "get the job done" have a certain look about them.
Those who have major self doubt or who feel defeated have
a different appearance.

Most parents, because of their own recollections of
childhood experience, or through their own education, believe it important for their children to develop a sense of
high SE. Praise for a child's accomplishment and reassurance, when some insecurity about ability or performance
is suspected, are generally assumed to be advisable practices to which parents should adhere. Even with the most
enlightened and careful parents, though, there are times

21

when parental comments or behavior make a child feel less confident or self assured. In those unfortunate situations, where children are subject to humiliating behavior by parents, or find themselves in situations where it is difficult to feel secure about what will happen next, virtually everyone agrees that these children may grow up with distorted estimates of SE. Some parents, who have consistently provided excellent care for each of their children, nevertheless note variations in levels of self assurance among their offspring.

We can probably agree that any of our life experiences may have an impact on how we value ourselves and therefore affect SE. Some days we feel more or less confident, often without any easily understood reason. At times we feel good about or think highly of ourselves, and at other times we may have negative feelings or think poorly of ourselves. Surprisingly, this variability of assessment may sometimes derive its momentum from even trivial provocations. Successful ventures tend to raise our feelings of SE. Praise from others about such accomplishments may serve as enhancement. Unsuccessful ventures usually produce lower feelings of SE. Criticism about such failures may exacerbate the condition. Such emotions may occur even when we know everyone fails at times, and even though we are usually successful at things.

Relationships often have an impact on our sense of SE. When we are fortunate enough to become friendly with someone we hold in high regard, our own sense of SE is enhanced. When we are held in high regard by peers or people who enjoy high prestige or power, we seem to like ourselves better. The enhancement born of love returned from one who is enormously desirable, is an incomparable sensation. Ecstacy produced by this kind of exchange includes wondrous feelings of high SE, as well as manifold emotions the poets describe much better than I.

It is particularly hurtful to be criticized, dismissed, abandoned, or disregarded by people we hold in high esteem. The pain is not as great when the people who perform these acts are not so highly regarded by us. When we are not respected by someone we value highly, we may become angry, but there also may be that unpleasant feeling associated with a reduced sense of SE.

Some childhood educators believe the attainment of high SE is the most important trait the educational process should strive to achieve for its students. Those who reason this way feel that unless children can attain this status, the accumulation of information and the learning of critical thinking skills will be harder to accomplish. Even at the traditional level of education, teachers have always recognized the benefit of rewarding their students with praise to help them gain confidence in themselves and their learning skills.

Therapists of many types try to instill a higher sense of SE in their patients. This may be through psychoanalysis, cognitive methods, support groups, meditation, and many other modalities of therapy. All of them assume that having good SE is a worthwhile and important goal to work towards, while of course also dealing with other types of problems patients may have.

Organized religions, through prayer, congregational activities, and rituals provide a climate and organization where people are encouraged to feel better about themselves. Social clubs provide an environment where being among others and participating in group activities may make people feel better about themselves, either through social acceptance by the group, or because of recognition for community service. Support of local sports teams, as alluded to in the introduction, is a major arena for the pleasure and perils relating to the feelings attendant to winning and losing.

So it appears our culture intuitively knows the importance of SE in our lives. It also seems generally understood that attaining or having a high level of SE is something positive and also feels good, and having low SE is not such a good thing and usually associated with a feeling we do not like.

The trend towards more self awareness and self absorption in some members of our culture has triggered many kinds of activities designed to help those people feel better or more satisfied in some way. Dropping out, drug use, indiscriminate sexual activity, greed, accumulation of material goods, and intensive exercise activities are some of the ways modern people have reacted to the stresses of living in our culture. There are many reasons why any individual might want to feel more comfortable and fulfilled in life, and though many of those needs may relate to evolutionary considerations, it is not my purpose to attempt to look at all of them. We will focus attention on that aspect of self awareness known as SE, and some of the behavior we exhibit in an attempt to feel better.

Numerous self help books guide the reader towards the means of acquiring high SE, because there is widespread need. Many people are unhappy because they feel they do not measure up. Our culture thrives on setting standards for acceptance into the various subdivisions of society. Competition exists in almost every aspect of daily life. The arenas for self comparison leaving the individual feeling deficient are numerous. This creates a fertile environment for publications designed to assist those looking for solutions to their problems. When there is no concensus as to how to understand and deal with a problem, various methods and programs proliferate. In my opinion, none of these have satisfactorily dealt with the essential aspects of SE.

There is also no standard definition of the term. The dictionary defines it as "pride in oneself" or "self respect."

Surprisingly, when one searches the psychiatric textbooks and classical writings of Freud, Jung, and Adler, one finds little discussion about self-esteem. The relatively new school of Self Psychology, made famous by Heinz Kohut, does look more at SE than prior theories did. This field believes the self and attendant SE, is a separate entity from the ego of Freud, and that it develops along a separate path than other parts of our psyches. Kohut theorized that we are born believing we are perfect beings and that the interplay of life events, and how we deal with them, determines how much narcissistic injury we sustain, and therefore how much our SE's are affected. His theory does not account for evolutionary mechanisms playing a role in SE. Anthony Stevens, a Jungian psychiatrist, is a leader in the new field of Evolutionary Psychiatry. This discipline endeavors to understand the origins of common disorders like depression, anxiety, bipolar syndrome, and others, by studying evolutionary archetypal patterns inherent in our brains. It theorizes that symptoms develop when the environment fails to meet certain human needs, based on these archetypes. In his books, Stevens discusses SE from the perspectives of what he calls rank and attachment theory. According to this belief, people develop pathologic alterations of SE when they suffer losses of significant relationships in their lives or experience reductions in status in a particular group. While this theory is predicated on evolutionary data and has merit in explaining possible derivations of psychological disease states, it limits discussion of SE issues to attachment and rank. It does not deal with moment to moment challenges animals and human face, or the relationship of those challenges to SE.

Other mental health experts in the field of clinical psychology have written extensively, but do not define SE in a way which relates it to a more basic part of our brain functioning, nor to what I believe to be its pervasive presence in our everyday lives.

Nathaniel Branden, Ph.D.,. a clinical and research psychologist, has authored a series of popular books on SE, and I think he comes closest to understanding how important the concept is in everyday life. His definition of SE talks about "confidence in the ability to think and cope with the basic challenges of life and confidence in being happy, the feeling of being worthy, deserving, entitled to assert our needs and wants and to enjoy the fruits of our efforts."

Throughout Branden's books he talks about the need to avoid comparing oneself to others to determine one's SE. He believes we should not be concerned with others' opinions of us but rather the feelings of good SE need to be generated from within, from an "individual's relationship to self." Based on his ideas, surrounding oneself with admirers cannot raise SE. Branden's notions depend on the conscious ability to think about and formulate high SE. In other words, if we have accomplished something which our thinking self is satisfied with, then we will have high SE. He does not believe in any innate or instinctual control of our feelings of SE.

As with other authors, Branden devotes attention to the effects of the types of parental upbringing which help to determine our SE. There are also references to SE being a powerful human need and that its absence, meaning low SE, impairs our ability to function in a rapidly changing complex world. He also makes the assumption that having high SE causes the individual to seek the stimulation of demanding goals. People with SE "do not seek to prove their value by measuring themselves against a comparative standard, their joy is in being who they are, not being better than someone else." He also believes the concept of SE does not exist for animals.

I believe the notable writers in all of the various fields dealing with SE have missed the concept that our feelings related to SE are derived from an ancient brain mechanism

I call the SE Switch. *This device is imagined as a powerful, built-in mechanism in all of us, placed there through the evolutionary process and operating within each of us all the time with the primary function of letting us know how we are doing from moment to moment.*

It is my guess this "Switch" exists, in some form, in the animal world, and is probably part of what we call instinct, enabling various creatures in their quest for survival. Genes probably account for the presence and basic functioning of this "Switch," which is capable of providing sublime feelings of pleasure and contentment, as well as awful feelings of despair and displeasure. This "Switch" may be activated by internal judgments of who we are, without necessarily comparing us to an outside standard, by comparison of ourselves to others, and by the evaluation of others, as well as a myriad other things and events which impact on us.

When "The Switch" is activated in the positive mode, there is an immense payoff of pleasurable feeling, so powerful it is impossible to miss. This payoff may at times become an end in itself, something which feels so good we may seek it out. Of course, sometimes while seeking there may be failure, and the payoff is an unpleasant one.

Tom Shroder of *The Miami Herald* wrote about the mysteries of golf on March 9, 1997, noting flashes of brilliance and a sense of the "real you" attending a good shot, and also the opposite attendant belief, quickly acquired, of "I stink" accompanying a poor shot. Anyone who has played golf is aware of these rapidly shifting emotions and of course, part of the game relates to the golfer's ability to overcome negative feelings. Part also relates to its addictive aspect, and the quest to hit brilliant shots, and become the "real you."

An editorial in *The New York Times* on November 19, 1994, discussed "the impossible task of ceasing to care." This piece related to the immense tug experienced each year by the writer to see the Alabama / Auburn football game, and the personal investment in the outcome of the game he noticed even though he was long removed from attending college, or having any practical thing to do with the University of Alabama. Many of us can relate to similar feelings of desperately wanting "our team to win," even when there is no measurable or logical reason that an adverse outcome should matter. Our identification with the team and the positive payoff of winning, in the form of pleasurable emotions, is what produces the "tug."

When in 1997 the Green Bay Packers returned home with the Lombardi Trophy after their Super Bowl victory, their bus was mobbed by adoring fans, even though the temperature stood at 19 degrees with bitter winds making it even more uncomfortable. Schools had closed early, workers took a holiday, the streets were lined six-deep to welcome the team home. In my opinion, the fans' reception and enthusiasm, even in terrible weather, took place because their SE switches were turned on in the strongly positive mode, creating the euphoria which led to this scene. The mutual pleasures and satisfactions experienced by the players and fans were of a magnitude too great to express in ordinary words, leading to the utterance of that time worn phrase: "That's what it is all about." These feelings were the payoff of The SE Switch.

Jon Kabat-Zinn, a leader in Insight Meditation, has stated that low SE is related to not seeing one's better parts, and that mindfulness enables more accurate perception of reality, which in turn improves one's SE. This implies that feelings of low SE are often simply related to not being fully in touch with oneself.

William James, the eminent 19th century psychologist, believed one's SE was determined by the formula [SE=success / pretentions,] implying that not only could one have feelings of high SE by virtue of a higher numerator, but also by having a small denominator, namely few expectations of success.

Stanley Coopersmith, a modern psychologist who has done extensive work in this field, felt that SE is defined by a personal judgment of worthiness expressed in the attitudes the individual holds towards himself, suggesting that a complex process looking at both outside and inside events leads an individual to feelings of SE.

Whether SE is internally generated, without the need for outside events to shape it, or determined by success or failure in our worldly endeavors, I believe it is always composed of a fluid set of feelings which may be modified at any given moment. Whether SE is governed by comparison of oneself with others, or by their opinions of us, it is affected *all the time* by factors activating the SE Switch.

I believe the model of a switch, selected for development by evolutionary pressures for survival, is a new means of understanding SE. I also believe such a model may account for many of the everyday feelings and experiences we all encounter, which were previously attributed to other phenomena. Pride, prestige, the need to "be right," arrogance and anger will be examined from this new perspective. Disorders of SE, and possible insights into healthier methods of dealing with emotions generated by the SE Switch, will also be discussed from the vantage point of this evolutionary device.

The origin of the SE Switch in the human animal will be described in the next two chapters. To understand this beginning, it will be necessary to review some of the science relating to the evolution of animal and human behavior.

Chapter 2

Evolutionary Psychology

"The tide of evolution carries everything before it, thoughts no less than bodies, and persons no less than nations."

George Santayana, 1920

The theory of natural selection, formally proposed by Charles Darwin in 1859, is so simple in concept it is hard to understand why none of the great thinkers of the ages came to it sooner. This is yet another example of the difficulty in understanding the most basic things about ourselves. Darwin's theory proposes: an organism's inherited traits, having provided some advantage for surviving in a particular environment, will tend to be passed on to future generations simply because the organism, by virtue of surviving, is more likely to produce offspring. These descendants, having inherited genetic material from their parents, are then more likely to also have the beneficial traits. Similarly, traits inherited through the genes not having the capacity to improve chances for survival, are eventually lost to future organisms, because death does not allow propagation. Hence, the traits observed in a plant or animal are present because they assisted prior generations with survival and therefore to have the potential to propagate new

31

generations. The giraffe's long neck enables it to eat otherwise unobtainable, high-up vegetation; the kangaroo's pouch allows it to carry its young safely while being free to move about and use its arms for other important activities.

It is important to understand that this theory, while specific in its genetic basis, is really in complete harmony with those notions proposing that learning and education are the essential methods by which humans become what they are. In fact, humans, especially human infants, have probably evolved through natural selection into incredibly able learning machines. Our ability to learn and benefit from our learning is not inconsistent with evolution having blessed us with the genetic traits to do this. I believe there is a constant interplay between our hard-wired, evolution-produced, structural brains, and our environment, creating a constantly changing unique individual from conception to death. Our brains have the ability to change constantly as we have life experiences, and to incorporate these experiences into the structural makeup of our brains. However, there probably remain basic kinds of human traits, which remain relatively stable throughout life and are common to all of us.

Our human nature cuts across all kinds of potential impediments against similarity. New Guinea tribes, never in touch with the outside world, smile and frown in the same ways civilized people do. Blind infants smile early in life at the same age seeing infants do. All humans utilize gramatic language, tend to care for our young, feel especially close and protective of immediate relatives, have romance at least in some form, have sexual competition and jealousy, and hierarchies of power and status regardless of the kind of society or degree of education within it. While Shakespeare probably understood these parts of human nature as well as anyone, it took evolutionary scientists to suggest that much of what is common to us as humans probably is related to our basic genetic makeup and the evolutionary mechanisms selecting out specific genes.

What is now more commonly called Evolutionary Psychology, rather than Sociobiology, studies our human nature from a unique perspective. This science examines us as individuals, families, groups, and societies, comparing us at times with other animals, and tries to discern what on a genetic or evolutionary basis makes us the way we are. DNA, present in the lowest forms of creatures, as well as being the basic components of our genes, influence organisms in many ways. The DNA directs how our bodies are formed. It also determines the particular functions cells, organs, and tissues in our bodies will be capable of performing. The information translated from DNA also determines the kind of brain and central nervous system we will have. Sperm and eggs are predominantly chromosomal materials comprised of genes. The genes are composed of DNA. It is this material given to us from our parents and passed on by us to our offspring which has so much to do with what kind of organisms we are, and therefore how we feel and behave.

Awakening in the morning, sleeping at night, sharing a meal with loved ones or friends are examples of basic activities we ordinarily take for granted. There must, however, be some rational explanation why most humans do these things, regardless of where they live or the kind of society they reside in.

Protection of our young at almost any cost is a basic human value. Ineffable as the primary colors, the emotions driving this instinctive behavior are not reducible to explanation. The agony of loss of loved ones is an equally powerful feeling. Words do not do the suffering justice. It is one of those sensations that needs to be experienced to understand its full measure. The various kinds of love from brotherly to romantic seem also to be universal human traits. Belief in spiritual aspects of humans, creation and enjoyment of music, art, literature, and myths are other examples appearing in all forms of humans around the world. Willful aggression or altruistic acts, like sacrificing one's life to protect home or homeland, patriotism, fear of strangers, and prejudice are other examples. Kindness towards the needy, generosity, greed and indifference, also seem to be universal human traits.

While it is difficult for many of us to relegate some of these almost sacred parts of our humanity to a genetic basis, there is good scientific evidence that it is so. Of the previously listed traits some are easily seen to have survival value to the individual organism and some do not appear to have direct benefit. The instinct to protect our young is a clear example of the former. Most parents have experienced the horrible emotion occurring when there is a threat of harm to their child.

Evolution has engineered the development of these protective phenomena via the structure of our DNA. Creation of and enjoyment of a Mozart symphony would not appear to have a direct survival benefit, but ages ago, when conditions were completely different, they probably did. Evidence shows that it took millions of years for our mammalian ancestors to evolve into humans. Musical capability may have had an advantage, for those with the trait, by virtue of being another method to communicate feelings in addition to spoken and written language. Music may also have helped to provide a means to bring people together in cooperation, enabling survival in difficult environments.

It is known that mutations, spontaneous and random changes in our genes, occur at the approximate rate of 100 per individual per generation. These events are predominantly caused by low level radiation we are exposed to by virtue of living on this planet. Internal events within our bodies also cause mutations. This means that if a mutation occurred in genetic material in a nonsexual cell in our body, that cells's function could change. This is so because the

DNA, comprising the genetic material, is the director of how the cell functions. A change in it alters what the cell does in the same way modifying the words in a poem or novel change its meaning. More importantly, if such a change takes place in a sexual cell, namely a sperm or egg producing cell, there would be the potential for a new trait to manifest itself once fertilization takes place and a new individual develops. This may or may not be beneficial for such an individual. Only its life experiences in its natural environment will determine the survival value of this new trait.

An evolutionary theory exists regarding the loss of skin pigment in the human species. It is believed that early humans, living in East Africa millions of years ago, probably had deeply pigmented skin. Vitamin D, necessary for proper bone growth and strength, was available to the individual primarily via its production in the skin. (It had not been added to milk in those days). For it to be produced, a chemical reaction requiring an adequate amount of sunlight was necessary. With the eventual migration of Homo Sapiens to the northern climates, where there was less sunlight, it is believed that dark skin, by its resistance to the effects of sunlight, could not create enough vitamin D to prevent bone fractures. This could be fatal to an early human in those times. Random mutation caused by cosmic radiation, or simply by an accident of replication of DNA, may have caused a decrease in the production of skin pigment for a particular individual or his offspring. While this change would make the skin more sensitive to sunburn and eventually more prone to skin cancer, it allowed more vitamin D to be synthesized by the skin. With more vitamin D available, there would be a lesser chance of bone injury, increasing the chances for survival. Those who did survive could procreate and pass on this new trait. This could account for that trait, light-colored skin, becoming more prevalent in the people inhabiting northern climates.

The normal production of sex cells or gametes involves the process known as meiosis. One half of an individual's genetic material, in both males and females, is randomly donated to these gametes. Because of the structural nature of chromosomes and their component genes, being paired and able to mix with and disconnect from partners in many ways, the makeup of each chromosome represented in the newly created sex cells is unique. When fertilization, or the joining together of egg and sperm, takes place, the genetic material mixes. This is the reason the same parents produce different children rather than the same one over and over again. While there are obvious similarities and resemblances among offspring, each individual is endowed with a unique genetic pedigree by virtue of this process. Once they inhabit an individual's body the genes remain remarkably stable. It has been estimated that it takes 20-50 generations for one to be replaced rather than just modified by a mutation. Currently, there is a tremendous amount of research being done to learn how to alter genes which cause disease, plus artificially providing new genes when that might be helpful in treating diseases.

While it seems easy to accept the notion of instinct in animals determining the way they behave, or their nature, it is not so easy to accept the same ideas about ourselves. For those who believe our human nature is determined solely by divine creation, there is no need to speculate about human instinct. But for many who still wonder about the origins of our nature, it may still be difficult to accept the notion that we are animals, and that much of our behavior, like animal instinct, is determined by programmed genetic mechanisms. The best evidence to support the belief that genes control the creation of our brains, and to a great extent our nature, involves studies of identical twins raised apart from each other. These represent near perfect experiments where identical genetic material exists in two people who also have completely different life experiences, education, parenting, etc.

The overwhelming findings in these studies point to similar tastes, interests, behavior, choices, and personalities of the two individuals. Usually those twins prefer the same kind of music, clothing, recreational activities, and often will choose the same kinds of members of the opposite sex as mates. This suggests that nature, through genetic endowment, has much more influence regarding our makeup than nurture or experience. There are many other kinds of scientific as well as common sense evidence that such is the case; the interested reader is referred to some of the literature listed in the bibliography for further understanding in this area.

This is not to suggest that an individual cannot make rational choices in the face of competing drives or urges, perform as a responsible citizen even when other feelings are present, or achieve more than others in the family or group from which he comes. The theory certainly does not propose there are such things as superior races or peoples or that political thinking requires that one group dominate another. It simply means much of our humanness comes from a long evolutionary process which has created the general kind of beings that we are. When Darwin put forth his theory, some automatically assumed that if the theory were true, then people ought to behave in a manner consistent with survival of the fittest, a dog-eat-dog kind of society. Darwin never suggested this, nor does his theory really require that conclusion. In fact, the theory provides an explanation for the most wonderful parts of our natures, because some of these traits helped humans survive rather than perish as a species.

Darwin did not suggest that all traits found in a species are specifically related to an improved ability to survive. Some may simply come along for the ride, so to speak, not playing any role in survival, but created as a by-product of a process producing other changes in the species. Stephen J. Gould, the eminent evolutionary writer, with Richard Lewontin, a Harvard biologist, described this phenomenon beautifully regarding the spandrels of San Marco, in the ceiling of St. Marks Cathedral in Venice. Spandrels are triangular panels which appear to have a unique design seeming to serve some special function for the overall structure. In fact, these spandrels are simply the consequence of building a dome supported by circular arches, created incidentally to another required structure rather than serving some roles themselves. They appeared, because of their unique shape, to have been designed by intention. Not everything we can describe about our natures or structure may be attributed to survival value. Some traits may exist solely because they are necessary consequences of others.

As mentioned, Dr. Wilson's treatise on Sociobiology, describing genetically determined causes for social behavior in animals and humans, created a furor with many evolutionary scientists. They felt this discipline was scientifically flawed and reductionistic, or overly simplified in terms of what is genetically determined. Some experts felt it left little room for learning, morality, or attainment of a spiritual life. Like Darwin's work, Wilson's has been misunderstood by some, perhaps their own SE getting in the way, because they did not formulate the theory first. Claims he never made are attributed to him. In fact, reading his works, one is struck by a sense of ethics and morality and his desire to see a more peaceful, less warlike and harmonious planet. He seems to believe that evolutionary process, through change of genetic material by natural selection, not only produced the aggressive, combative parts of our nature, but also the kind, caring, love, respectful, and creative parts we like to believe makes us unique.

The evolutionary process has created in plants and animals the most complex things which exist on our planet, all with a system of mechanisms or internal signals which advise the organism how to behave in certain situations. The types of outward appearances of various creatures and their particular kinds of behavioral patterns are almost without limit in variety. While some of these features appear to be peculiar only to a particular species, we humans can see comparisons to our own behavior at times. For example, the wonderful plumage of certain male birds evolved as a means of attracting females. At the same time, the females evolved an appreciation for that plumage. Via internal signals we call instinct, the female would know which bird's plumage was more desirable to her and therefore which male might be the best to mate.

Human males with certain attributes are more sexually appealing to women who have evolved to be receptive to those features. Psychological studies have shown that men with broad shoulders, prominent chests, and powerful looking legs are generally more sexually appealing to women, other things being equal. When women are asked why this is so, they offer no clear reason other than feelings experienced. This phenomenon is probably produced by complex brain circuitry able to make such evaluations and produce feelings which are interpreted as desires.

Internal signals or instincts are what guide the behaviors. These signals have evolved by production of genes through the evolutionary process, and it is these signals, along with learning from past experience, that direct the organism toward choices promoting the survival of those genes. In mammals and primates, many of these signals take the form of emotions, to be discussed in later chapters. What at first blush looks like a production necessarily choreographed with a grand design, the process of natural selection operates by chance, and has created living things of great complexity with all their internal signals or instincts. The SE Switch, originally a complex device for survival, I believe is one of those mechanisms.

Chapter 3

The SE Switch

"Science is nothing but trained and organized common sense."

Thomas Henry Huxley, 1870

Why should a SE Switch evolve? Why should natural selection have, by random activity over millions of years, created a mechanism so powerful in its effect on individuals? Unless, like Gould's spandrels, it came along for the ride, we must assume there was survival value for organisms with this feature, or else it would have gradually been lost, rather than retained in humans to the grand extent it exists.

Some popular writers of SE believe the concept does not apply to lower animals. Scientific evidence, however, strongly suggests that SE issues are important for animals. What is described by scientists as "resource holding potential" is the mechanism which enables an animal to know instinctively how it is doing in a particular situation or environment. In our previous example of male lions vying for a female, natural selection or the evolutionary process has built into these lions the ability to determine, without a fight to the death, which would win if it were actually fought. We might call this intuition, if we were talking about human behavior. Body appearance and body language, perceptions of strength, agility, cunning, determination, and courage are quickly and automatically computed by each of the lions, causing one to back off, conceding the female prize to the more dominant animal.

What scientists call the animal's "resource holding potential" is that internal brain mechanism which allowed the lions to know what to do in a potentially life and death situation, to insure the best outcome for themselves. It is an unconscious self-assessment of the animal's sense of relative fitness for a particular task, or comparison of itself to other animals either of same or different species. *"Resource holding potential" is the equivalent of the animal's SE and the SE Switch is the proposed evolutionary device governing it.*

There is much scientific research literature on the topic of survival instincts, but it is not clear what kinds of internal signals the animals perceive helping them to make decisions. It is my guess that the dominant lion experiences sensations similar to what humans feel when SE is very high, namely feelings of confidence, assuredness, enthusiasm, telling him, so to speak, to proceed with his endeavor. In other words, the dominant lion felt good, emboldened, encouraged within the context of being a lion. The less dominant lion, having automatically assessed his "resource holding potential," or SE, felt insecure, frightened, uncertain, perhaps even sickly, experiencing internal signals telling him to cease and desist, to stop the encounter and leave defeated but alive.

In this example, the evolutionary process produced only winners, because the less dominant lion stays alive, possibly to succeed in another encounter. The dominant lion gains access to the female who is now blessed by having a sexual mate of greater prowess, perhaps helping to insure that her new cubs will have traits similar to the father's. This makes it more likely those cubs will survive hostile environments and eventually be able to pass on their own genes.

The evolution of mechanisms to send emotional messages to animals, guiding them in their drive to survive, was produced by natural selection. Many other mechanisms probably developed by this random process, but simply failed, and so were not brought along in next generations because the owners of those systems did not live to procreate. This system, like the internal combustion engine, intentionally created by man to meet his needs, has withstood the test of time, found still in much of the animal kingdom, and in humans. Such is obviously also the case for most of the organ systems in mammals, like the cardiovascular, pulmonary, gastrointestinal, urinary, musculoskeletal, endocrine, etc. These have evolved over millions of years, and become very efficient in keeping animals alive and allowing them to procreate. Within each of them, there are many components that have evolved to allow the success of the whole system.

A direct example in the central nervous system is known as REM sleep, the cycle in our sleep when we dream. REM is short for rapid eye movement, an observable phenomenon occurring while dreaming. Most experts agree this kind of mechanism has evolved to enable an animal both to rest and also use the time to process and integrate new information the senses have taken in that day, helping the animal learn and use such information for the future. Some scientists believe that dreams are really our witnessing of this process of sorting out new information and comparing it with old, stored memories in our brains. Having this feature in the brain allows more complex function without the need for a larger brain, something limited by the size of a mother's pelvis. During REM sleep, our bodies are temporarily paralyzed, the muscles in a state of relaxation. This system could not work as well if an animal were more of a subject of predation, and it turns out that humans, not often such subjects, have the largest percentage of REM sleep.

If the SE Switch exists in animals, it probably involves complex mechanisms in the brain which have little to do with thinking, conscious choice, or decision making as humans know them. As with instincts, these are sets of signals in their brains which cause them to react in certain ways. The amygdala, hippocampus and limbic system in humans process messages and create what we call emotions. Evolutionary theory suggests that development of mammalian infants, totally dependent on nursing for survival, required mechanisms that protected against separation from the mother, a potentially calamitous situation. Sea otter mothers are known to carry their pups in the dangerous ocean environment for one year, placing all other aspects of their interests after this primary need. Most human mothers have built-in, incredibly strong emotional drives to protect their young. Natural selection produced structures in the brain capable of sending strong emotional signals to protect against separation of mother and infant, as well as other dangerous situations. While those animals obviously cannot tell us how they are feeling, it is likely they experience similar feelings to us, because they have the same kinds of brain structures known to be the source from which emotions arise in humans. Those feelings, generated from moment to moment, depending on what is occurring in the environment, are perceived at some level by the animal and direct the animal to a particular behavior. The sensation may be as simple as a sense of peace and safety, enabling the animal to rest and let down its guard, or one of sheer terror, telling the animal to run or fight.

The power or urgency of a particular set of emotional signals in an animal is relative, and the genetic equipment producing the signals evolved for different purposes. For example, the feelings a predator experiences in telling him to pursue his prey as a next meal probably are of a different

44

level from those messages sent to the prey, which may enable him to escape from becoming a meal. The predator only loses a meal if he is unsuccessful, while the prey loses his life if he is unsuccessful. The kinds of internal signals are probably similar for the predator and prey, emotion being the mediator of the action to be taken by each animal. What is different is the kind of emotional message sent, the prey feeling fright and desperation, and the predator hungry, aggressive, and determined. This use of emotion developed as a major mechanism for survival in higher forms of animals, and the structures of the brain governing those functions are present in all mammals.

I believe the SE Switch probably resides within the part of the brain called the limbic system, which generates emotions in mammals. Various kinds of emotional signals are probably always being experienced by the animals, which help them know how to behave in feeding, playing, living together in groups, attaining power, fighting, courting, mating, parenting, and other behaviors.

The SE Switch is the main mechanism for the animal to determine its "resource holding potential," or ability to tell by emotional messages whether it is up to certain tasks or not. Like the emotion related to separation of mother and child, designed to protect the child from catastrophe, the SE Switch provides another kind of emotional signal designed to keep the animal alive. It tells the animal whether it has the capabilities to leap across a divide, or whether to fight or withdraw. It tells the animal if it has a realistic chance to mate with an attractive member of the opposite sex, and whether it can compete with members of its own sex for that mate. It probably also tells the animals in a pack who should lead and who should follow, who should have first access to food when it is found or killed, and also if a particular place is safe.

The SE Switch is another accomplishment of the evolutionary process whereby utilization of a different kind of central nervous system function, namely that of emotion, provides animals with more information in their pursuit of survival. By "inventing" emotion, the need to create more highly specialized sensory organs like eyes and ears to improve chances for survival were obviated. Such organs would have undoubtedly taken much more time to evolve than did the addition of new circuitry in an already existing brain. The limbic lobe was also an efficient use of brain space and the already existing machinery of the primary sensory organs. The development of the SE Switch, the animal's method of determining its capabilities, was another example of the efficiencies evolution often accomplishes.

In our early human like ancestors, as in other mammals, the SE Switch probably functioned mostly in the realm of survival. The emotional signals helped the individual know which battles to fight and when it was safe to attempt to slay an animal. Positive signals would tell the individual to advance and venture forth, and negative ones to back off or hide. Ancestors who were risk takers and successful may have been selected out and produced more offspring like them. Those whose SE Switches might tend to fire in the positive mode to encourage boldness, when others may have been less courageous, might be more likely to kill dangerous prey, or find a new, safer, and better home, or perhaps a more desirable mate. If those switches misled them into catastrophe, then those individuals would not survive.

Emotional messages from an SE Switch could also have helped in protection of the young by sending signals to the mother, allowing her to judge which other early humans it would be safe to be near. To know one's "resource holding potential" was to know when and when not to take risks.

Perhaps most importantly, the SE Switch may have enabled protohumans to know how to organize in groups. The ability to size up each other's strengths and weaknesses would be a requisite for determining who could best lead and who might be better off following. It would also enable cooperation rather than never-ending belligerence and fighting, a trait aiding group survival by working together towards a common goal rather than at individual purposes. SE Switches which functioned well for individuals would enable them to determine where they fit in, and may have been a key factor in determining how successful a group would be. This ability to organize into well functioning groups has been considered by evolutionary scientists one of the major reasons Homo Sapiens has become such a successful species.

Chapter 4

Traditional Views of SE

*"Oh, the powers of nature! She knows what we need,
and the doctors know nothing"*
                                   Benvenuto Cellini, 1558

Clinicians who deal with SE issues with patients realize there is tremendous variation of general levels of SE from person to person as well as within each individual. Also, many complex factors affect the development of an individual's own SE. Parental attitudes and behavior towards their children clearly play a role in the process as do one's own experiences of success or failure in dealing with people, and the problems related to confronting them. Our brains are able to store, with great emotional tone, our previous history of victories and defeats. Praise or criticism of performance by others may be powerfully remembered especially if that judgment came from a person held in high regard. Acceptance or rejection by highly respected groups may also have powerful effects on the individual's SE.

There exist many clinical means of grading one's SE, from designated rating scales to simple clinical judgements made by experts in the field. Many psychiatric disorders have, as part of them, alterations in SE. Correlates of psychiatric illness tend to develop in those people who seem to have intrinsically low SE. Depression and low SE have been strongly linked, each leading to the other in some cases. People with chronically low SE are some of the hardest patients to treat. The pervasive feelings of not being up to many tasks produces an unhappy state of existence, which can be refractory to treatment. Membership in cult groups, violent behavior, and addictions are common among those unfortunate people who have the chronic misery associated with low SE.

Therapists face particular challenges in trying to treat people with chronically low SE. Practitioners may be faced with alternating idealization and disparagement, depending on how their own behavior is perceived. If these types of patients believe not enough respect or consideration has been paid them, they may become very angry, making the treatment process more difficult.

Some people with low SE find themselves too anxious to engage in any activity involving competition, especially if it has to do with members of their own sex. The feelings attendant to low SE may also make them feel so inhibited, they do not trust themselves in normal social interactions. Activities like being with friends, participating in an organization, or attending church may be too uncomfortable for them. Psychiatrists trained in the classical theory may diagnose Oedipal disorder related to unhealthy interactions of mother and child, not allowing the child to develop a normal sense of SE, i.e., when a mother does not allow her child to feel secure and safe in her presence. Therapists who subscribe to self psychology may believe many of these patients suffered narcissistic injuries in childhood, damaging a supposed perfection beyond repair.

People with so-called healthy levels of SE see setbacks as temporary and, even if momentarily overwhelmed emotionally, trust their ability to overcome the problem and are rapidly back on track feeling confident. Those who are rarely affected by issues of SE have "unselfconscious individuality," according to Mihaly Csikszentmihalyi, the author of "Flow." As he described, these people have the ability not to fall apart when external conditions turn threatening. They are neither thrilled by success nor overwhelmed by failure. As the famous Kipling plaque in the Wimbledon Clubhouse reminds tennis competitors, "treat both those imposters the same."

Some people experience little emotion related to issues of SE. It does not appear to matter much to them how they are viewed by others, nor do they evaluate their own performances or abilities with much feeling. While these people are seemingly protected from some of the agonies of the feelings of low SE, they may have other problems relating to a deficiency of emotional signals in general.

Then there are those with a falsely inflated sense of SE, usually because parents have sent inappropriate messages about their prowess in a particular field, or inflated them with notions of "specialness" as human beings. These people may have greatly exaggerated emotional responses regarding feelings of SE when certain incidents occur, becoming too elated at something which reflects well upon them, and clearly upset for "too long" when they experience a failure or embarrassment.

As described, there are many varieties of psychiatric disorders relating to problems of SE. A large literature exists regarding diagnosis and treatment of these kinds of disorders, and many different types of therapeutic approaches to deal with these problems. Classical analysis and attempts at revisiting Oedipal issues relating to early hostile competition with a parent, attempts to restore the integrity of the "self," through understanding of painful childhood incidents, and behavior modification designed to bolster SE are some of the traditional therapeutic techniques used in treating patients with low SE. Group therapy may also provide certain dynamics which help those with damaged SE feelings see that others have similar or worse feelings. Freud recognized the improvement in SE for patients who experienced spiritual sensations related to religious practice. Faith in god and efforts to achieve moral virtue are believed by some experts to serve as sources of power for an individual and may create a psyche which feels relatively impenetrable to the ordinary threats of everyday life.

Studies have demonstrated that patients who engage in meditative techniques notice an improvement in their levels of SE. When people feel connected to a deeper part of themselves, they often see themselves having more value, and thereby have higher baseline levels of SE. This may be a mechanism of bypassing the usual ego involvement in SE issues and allowing a different pathway in the brain to operate. Yoga and other alternative type therapies may also play a useful role in assisting those suffering chronically from low SE.

This chapter has provided a brief tour of how modern therapists deal with issues relating to SE. Most recognize this is an important arena, and much insight has been gained into understanding the disorders associated with alterations of SE, and how to treat them. What has been missing from the diagnostic and potential therapeutic approaches is the notion underlying the subject of this book. This idea proposes ancient but vibrant brain mechanisms whose purpose is to generate feelings related to SE. These feelings, experienced as intense emotion, have a pervasive effect on even the normal individual, by virtue of their evolutionary endowment.

It is my contention that the SE Switch is always operating, informing us of how we are doing. Therapists have not worked with this concept from that perspective, namely understanding there is a constant stream of information coming to the organism, which, by design, is automatically evaluated regarding fitness. This process needs to be understood for what it is and capitalized on. SE should not just be recognized as a condition, but rather as a more integral part of everyday human function.

The built-in SE Switch has played a large role in how we have gotten to where we are as humans. Instead of focusing on whether SE is high or low, appropriate or defective, we need to see how intrinsic to the human experience it is, how it often motivates what we do or don't do even when operating normally.

There exists a vast part of human experience, both mundane and metaphysical, which I believe is related to the operation of this switch. We have simply looked past the obvious regarding this notion. To repeat, simple concepts, like this one, may be the hardest first to see, and then to understand.

Chapter 5

The SE Switch in Operation

"If you have built castles in the air,
  your work need not be lost;
  that is where they should be.
Now put the foundations under them.

Thoreau, 1854

"We're number 1, we're number 1." Arms and fingers thrusting towards the heavens, bodies and faces thrilling to the notion, visible ecstacy, unbridled joy, absolute fulfillment and satisfaction. A college team has won the NCAA tournament.

What kind of mental state is this? Thousands of young and old are celebrating the victory of "their" team. We have all seen this happen, and many have been fortunate enough to enjoy these sublime pleasures themselves. Why should a victory by a local sports team create such emotion within us? On a practical basis, no material change has occurred. Unless one has won a bet or has a financial interest in the team, there is no obvious reward. Also, in most cases, there probably has been no direct relationship with the players or coaches. Work, family relationships, most social relationships, taxes, political realities probably have not changed.

Religious or spiritual matters probably have not been affected by the sports victory either. So what accounts for such a profound emotional experience?

It is my belief that while many factors are at play in such a situation, the main factor producing the ecstatic feelings is the SE Switch. The individual identifies with the local team. It is part of himself. Its victory is his victory. Winning represents validation to the individual that the team, and therefore *he*, was up to the task. The team competed successfully and therefore so did *he*. The team has the "resource holding potential" to accomplish the task, and therefore so did *he*. The very powerful message of ecstacy, produced by the SE Switch, was experienced by that individual as a signal with meaning. This immensely pleasurable sensation, created by the random chance of the evolutionary process, tells him the competitive endeavor was not only worthwhile but something to be attempted again rather than abandoned.

The ecstacy is a payoff from the SE Switch. Originally evolved to help the organism to know when to take chances, when to be cautious or submissive, it activates today with the same profoundly dramatic feelings for your team winning a game as it did for an early human perhaps engaging in a life and death circumstance, and prevailing. The evolutionary process produced information to help the organism to know "what to do next time," this ecstactic feeling not easily forgotten or ignored.

I think few would argue about our human ability to make and remember associations. Many psychological experiments and studies demonstrate how we can be conditioned to respond to particular stimuli. Smells have particularly strong associations with events of the past. Artifacts from our past personal lives are often associated with strong emotional feelings of nostalgia. Unhappy childhood experiences, like being bitten by a dog, may create lifelong feelings of fear of all animals. So the ecstacy experienced when "our" team wins will have strong and well-remembered associations for us with that event. Those conscious and unconscious recollections may add to the attraction of "the game," the next time "our" team competes.

In this example of the local team winning the crucial game, we see that the SE Switch provides a positive payoff for the fan who has chosen to be in the struggle with his team, and who has won. He has received the message in the form of a reward telling him how capable his team is and also perhaps how capable he is. We will return to this particular issue later.

The amazingly powerful pull upon the fan to watch the contest probably has to do with the positive payoff which comes with success. It is not uncommon for men to sacrifice many things in order to watch "the game." Despite the logical notion that the time might better be spent with spouse, family, creative endeavors, recreational activity, reading, pursuit of the arts, study, and other kinds of more worthwhile activities, the average fan feels compelled to watch the game. Most wives have learned to understand the power of this drive and no longer try to oppose it. Professional sports franchises certainly know the powerful nature of the draw to support and watch the local team. University and college teams bank on devotion to alma mater. The business interests attendant to sports teams can depend on fan support. It is almost unwavering. In spite of players who behave like spoiled children, owners of professional teams who care only about the bottom line, the teams still enjoy the support of the fans. Logic would dictate that fans would become cynical and less interested in professional sports, yet the opposite is true. The best explanation for their continued interest and loyalty, I believe, is the operation of the SE Switch. Its potentially positive feelings are just too hard to pass up.

We perceive the team as ours, as part of ourselves, and hence its exploits are ours. The players also become part of us. We learn much about them, their personal lives, their mannerisms, habits, strengths, weaknesses. In most cases, we have never met them, but we feel kin to them. They become important parts of our lives, even though they probably care very little about us or our real families. While watching "the game," we give them encouragement, as we would our children or spouses. We may become angry with them when they fail to perform to our expectations. In the same way we experience ecstacy for a personal accomplishment, like getting an "A" on a difficult exam in school, we feel this way when our team succeeds. That great roar of the crowd when our team has done something well is the collective expression of the thrill we have experienced when our SE switches turn on in the positive mode. We are rejoicing in the same way as if we had hit a perfect golf shot or had an epiphany about a problem long pondered, or if we were rewarded a million years ago for taking risk in pursuit of a mate and succeeding.

Let's look now at some of the vignettes I described in the introduction to the book. We have already analyzed the lions and talked about sports and fans.

A beautiful woman grooming herself in the morning is operating on several levels. At once, she is simply performing some hygiene for cleanliness and health. She is also preparing to comply with social expectations regarding appearance, and attempting to achieve certain results having to do with her own measurement of what her appearance means to her and her best guess as to what it means to others. If she is normal, she cares at least a little about the nature of her appearance. Intellectually, she knows it may have something to do with how she is treated by people, and perhaps to her success or lack of it in certain endeavors. At a deeper and more meaningful level, a judging process is underway by which she evaluates her appearance, determining if she meets her own criteria for looking her best, and experiencing special kinds of feelings

58

as she proceeds. The emotional experience will reinforce the simple sensory perceptions of how she looks. This automatic process also has her judging her appearance compared to other females she will encounter, and perhaps also to standards held by society. She will also, unconsciously, be evaluating herself based on "built-in" standards inherent in our brains which cause us to decide whether a female is beautiful or not. Psychological studies have determined designations of "beautiful" are generally associated with particular kinds of facial features.

In our example, the lady has feelings of satisfaction upon completion of her preparation. The SE Switch has turned on in the positive mode, unleashing those limbic lobe neurological messages in her brain which make her feel happy with herself, confident, motivated to go forward into the day's challenges, and all other things being equal probably optimistic and cheerful as well. Of course, even in this scenario, where an attractive female has been chosen to make a point, this particular "person" may have all kinds of other problems and issues producing feelings and emotions dominating the SE messages I have alluded to. Perhaps while being satisfied about her appearance, she is worried about the welfare of one of her children, or has injured her back and is in pain. Clearly, in those cases, many emotions occur at once, producing a conflicting set of feelings rather than the simple confident and pleasing sensation noted in the example.

We are too complex to think, at any given moment, that only one "switch" or emotion will manifest in us, or be the dominant emotion. Powerful emotions, their nature governed by the SE Switch, guide us into certain kinds of behavior when other major feelings are not competing. In our example of the attractive lady grooming herself, if she is not being impacted by other major issues, and if her internal calculations regarding her appearance turn the SE Switch to the positive mode, she will probably feel some of the kinds of positive emotions previously noted. A silent witness would say that she looked pleased and confident.

This same lady, because of the positive payoff of emotions associated with her grooming, will also, all other things being equal, look forward to the next grooming session, simply because it felt so good. We tend to do things which bring pleasure and positive results and avoid those that don't. The SE Switch does not simply tell us how we are doing at a given moment; it also tells us by the type of payoff whether a particular activity is one to be repeated in the future. Our evolved ability to make associations of events with emotions "teaches" us what are worthwhile activities.

Grooming is an activity prevalent in the animal kingdom, especially in mammals, and probably has some survival advantage. The concept of attractiveness is basic to the whole notion of sexual reproduction, so it is not surprising our attentions would turn to that issue as human beings. How attractive we are may help us decide many things; thus activities and issues related to attractiveness are major components of our everyday human endeavors. Billions of dollars and years of efforts are expended in our society in trying to look attractive. The SE Switch has accomplished the dual purpose of telling her she is competing well in the attractiveness game, and that the grooming itself is worthwhile. She will probably continue to have both pleasures.

In the example of the elderly, retired FBI worker, the victim of an old scam regarding her bank account, we can imagine the feelings of embarrassment, self anger, humiliation, and unhappiness she must have felt. To have worked her whole career in law enforcement should have provided the experience to be more cynical and careful than the next person. While aware of many kinds of criminal activities, nothing in this realm had happened to her before, nor had she made such a mistake in judgement about another person.

This patient is someone who has always exhibited "normal" self-esteem from a medical vantage point, not having problems with sadness, depression, interpersonal situations, competing, etc. Apparently, the negative feelings of SE generated by the misjudgment she made were intolerable to her. The fact that she knew herself to be intelligent, experienced, and also trained in recognizing scams, probably generated even more intense feelings by her particular SE Switch. In this circumstance, the SE Switch perhaps sent messages doubtfully useful for the future, but activated automatically because of the stimulus, and produced intense feelings of low SE. The sickeningly empty feelings associated with the SE Switch firing in the negative mode were too difficult to bear for her normal everyday functioning.

Several things might have occurred in the midst of these feelings. First, she could have just experienced them, and they probably would have gradually extinguished. She might have become angry, despondent or depressed. What apparently happened, though, was she simply decided to place the blame elsewhere, on society and law enforcement. This well known psychological mechanism, sometimes called projection, made her feel better. By turning her negative feelings about herself to another object, namely society and law enforcement, she got rid of the negative emotions from the SE Switch which made her feel so badly. She could feel good about herself again about this incident since it "really wasn't my fault," a psychological mechanism probably not as old as the SE Switch, but very effective. Now she could convince herself that she really did not fail, the bad thing was not her doing. Instead of simply telling her doctor how embarrassed she was in falling for the scam, a declaration which probably would have been met by her physician with great empathy and concern, she came armed with a solution to the SE Switch, one the physician could see through, but support, hopefully to her long term benefit.

A similar phenomenon is demonstrated by an article written by Leonard Garment in the Oct. 19, 1999, issue of *The New York Times*. Mr. Garment was counsel to President Nixon and is Jewish. He has impeccable credentials and enjoyed great integrity through the Watergate scandal to the present. The article in question was written regarding the latest revelations of Nixon's overt Anti-Semitism as disclosed in tapes recently released by The National Archives. While noting that Nixon's statements were "indefensible," Garment proceeded to defend them anyway, arguing that since the statements were made in private, a different standard of judgement needed to be applied than if made in public. Why would a lawyer of such high prestige risk writing such a self contradictory article?

The answer would appear to lie in the predicament of a Jew working for an obviously Anti-Semitic politician. Garment most likely felt challenges to his pride and SE when more embarrassing information about Nixon's hatred of Jews became public. Why did he continue to work for the President if he knew of Nixon's prejudice? Would not someone of high integrity be expected to resign? Since he did not resign and because he offered no higher explanation for continuing his service, he suffered symptoms from the same kind of dilemma facing the FBI worker. The negative SE messages were too uncomfortable to deal with. The SE Switch had performed its work, letting him know he had not done so well. Garment attempted to regain his SE by writing an article rationalizing Nixon's shortcomings in an effort to make himself look less suspect. While he may have felt better for writing it, I doubt it accomplished the goal of convincing others.

An unusual form of joy in "winning" is demonstrated in the example of the Howard University Law School Class.

Having been the object of racial bigotry for hundreds of years, and having been treated as inferior, is enough stimulus to create a dramatic increase in activity for anyone's SE Switch. The response to being treated in an arrogant manner, in our species, is that of universal anger, mistrust, and wariness towards those committing the offense. When a person or persons treat us in a way which says "I am superior to you," or "you are not my equal," we take a strong offense against that person and dislike him vehemently. We would certainly not trust that person to make a fair decision about something which would have an impact on us. We tend to trust people who treat us with respect. The business world learned long ago how important that notion is in selling any product or service, that someone ordinarily will not buy if he is not treated respectfully. Some eastern cultures hold this requirement high for any kind of personal or commercial transaction.

In the Simpson case, most black people did not believe the police or prosecutors had treated Simpson fairly because blacks have been treated arrogantly and with disdain by many in our society for hundreds of years, and clearly racism still exists. According to the polls, blacks believed the police had planted incriminating evidence in this case, even though most others agreed that it was unlikely they could have done so. Notwithstanding practical reasons to suspect police malfeasance, I believe most black people felt this black football hero was innocent, because that belief helped their own SE.

Since many blacks felt kin to him, more pleasant and acceptable feelings generated by their own SE Switches would be turned on by still believing in his virtues. As with the example of teams, and the individuals on those teams for whom we root and identify, our emotional investment in them seems to require that we hold them in the highest regard. We love our heroes and are devoted to them. We expect them to behave heroically on our behalves. For the law students to think this football hero had committed atrocious crimes probably would have turned their SE switches to the negative mode generating those sickening, unpleasant feelings which are so hard to deal with. There was a powerful force operating to leave the SE Switch on in the positive mode, because the opposite would be so painful.

The black law school students had clearly made the choice, perhaps unconsciously, perhaps not, to believe in and support Simpson, and when the verdict was read, they uniformly stood and cheered exuberantly for his acquittal. Was it because they were black and therefore automatically partisan, or was it strictly a political victory? I don't believe it was either. Did they think he was above the law? I do not think so. Did they believe they were getting even? Probably not. Especially in a group studying law, and in a group who had a high level of intelligence and attained advanced education, I believe there had to be more basic, emotionally driven forces at play.

For Simpson to have enjoyed their support during his prosecution, and for the students to experience their own feelings of joy at his acquittal, I believe, required the forces of the SE Switch to be at work. The SE Switch made it easier for the students to continue to believe in him and then it also fired forcefully when he [they], won. The SE Switch stayed in the positive mode throughout the course of this ordeal, allowing the students to feel better about themselves by continuing to feel good about Simpson.

We do not acquire our heroes easily. They need to accomplish what we consider to be great achievements for us to believe in their power and ability. When they have proven themselves, however, we allow them a special place in our minds and then in our society. Our SE Switches, always critically judging and evaluating, accept the hero because he is on "our side," thus making us feel better about ourselves. It makes us believe we are more powerful and capable. Once the hero has achieved this stature in our brains, it may be virtually impossible to ignore other information which might destroy the wonderful feelings the hero and the SE Switch have conspired to create. No one wants to feel nauseated or unwell. Brutality, cruelty, even arrogance might get overlooked if the SE Switch is in the positive mode sending us pleasant messages instead.

There are virtually limitless examples of how the SE Switch could operate in our everyday lives: in our relationships with coworkers, family, friends, significant others, business people, service providers, civic and religious groups, political groups, golf partners, etc. Rather than create a list, we will look, in subsequent chapters, at some other kinds of behavior we may all exhibit, or have to deal with, and what the relationship of these to the SE Switch may be. We will also look at some specific aspects of our human nature and try to see them from a somewhat different perspective.

Chapter 6

Pride and Prestige

"Pride is said to be the last vice the good man gets rid of."

Benjamin Franklin 1744

Bobby Inman is a retired four star admiral. In 1994, he was nominated by the President to become Secretary of Defense. Admiral Inman had been Deputy Director of the Central Intelligence Agency in a prior administration. He had been a savvy Washington veteran, widely respected. While apparently having ambivalence about taking the job, he accepted the offer, believing his Senate confirmation would be an easy process. He had gone through four of them in the past without a problem.

Very early into the confirmation process in the Senate, some questions and mild criticisms of his past decisions and choices were raised. He also was challenged in ways which had not occurred in his prior hearings. Without warning, Admiral Inman called a news conference, where he withdrew from the nomination, attacked his critics in the Senate and press, and accused them of trying to ruin his reputation in a frenzy of "modern McCarthyism." Not even the most sensitive of the media thought the Admiral had been abused in any way, but he felt his character and integrity were being attacked. His colleagues were baffled by his defensiveness and attack on the process of confirmation. All were at a loss to explain how a seasoned player in Washington, accustomed to its ways, could accept a nomination for a high post in the President's Cabinet and then withdraw with a seemingly inappropriate attack on Congressmen who were raising routine questions necessary to discharge their responsibilities.

What happened here? There is no evidence the Admiral suffered from any mental problem, and if he simply had changed his mind about wanting the job, there was no need for an attack on his questioners. He could have just gracefully bowed out. But he felt compelled to spend one hour in front of the cameras defending himself and attacking the people and system who were reviewing his fitness for confirmation.

While there were probably many different factors contributing to his behavior, I would speculate that a major one was the Admiral's pride and self respect were being threatened. If so, his SE Switch must have sent signals to him which were so unpleasant he had to take action. Recall that it is postulated that this switch is poised to tell us how we are doing at all times, and also at any given moment in time. It is there to protect us from injury, and to let us known when it is safe to proceed. Someone at Inman's station in life would have achieved enough successes over the years so that it should take quite a threat to turn the SE Switch on in the negative mode.

But no one is completely immune to attacks on character or integrity, and if there is a perception that such an attack is taking place, the SE Switch may believe this might represent a defeat to the organism, and send the kind of messages which make the organism withdraw to safety.

All of us expect a certain level of respect from those we deal with. We also, consciously or unconsciously, behave in ways which say we are concerned with our stature and relative position in the various groups of which we are members. If we are normal, we take pride in ourselves and expect others to recognize our value, whether we are retired four star Admirals engaged in a Senate confirmation hearing, or everyday people doing ordinary things.

For example, our choices of clothing are determined by many factors, but prominent among those factors is the notion of whether the clothing expresses to others our sense of ourselves. This necessarily requires that we have evaluated who and what we are, what we would like to be, and compared ourselves to certain accepted standards. Like it or not, fashions and styles have come into existence in all societies. I won't attempt here to deal with the derivation of those particular expressions of human nature other than to recognize their prevalent and major roles in many of our lives. We all have to make choices of how to dress, and therefore how to be seen by ourselves and others. Wearing clothing with a style representative of a particular group allows us to feel we have become one of its members. Undoubtedly, there is something about that category of people we admire or hold in high esteem and so dressing that way elevates us into that group. If it is classic business dress, then we are business men; if elegant high fashioned women's attire, then we are also elegant and high fashioned; if a white lab jacket, then we are doctors; if casual, then we are a member of the group which does not take everything so seriously and is capable of being laid-back and at ease.

How we clothe ourselves tells us and others about our level of prestige and pride. It is important because it tells us how we feel about how "we fit," and our level of competency to be in a particular group. It also sends the message that we want to be seen in a particular light, most likely one which commands respect. Police and military uniforms are the most obvious examples, but I believe the same concept exists for tennis dresses and men's blazers. The wearer of the clothing, at some level, wants acceptance and recognition for how he looks both from himself and from those who see him. If you have guessed I am talking about the SE Switch, I am happy you have made the association. It monitors the environment and then sends us the messages we interpret as pride and prestige.

Where we live, what kind of home we live in, the kind of car we drive also has a lot to do with prestige and respect. There are of course multiple factors which determine what choices we make. Factored into these choices is the element of how we feel the particular home measures up in relation to our own sense of self-worth and how we believe that home will effect others' notions of how they view us and, therefore, how much respect they will have for us. Where one lives; the state, city, county, neighborhood, street, carries with it a whole set of feelings which are related to judgments about how powerful, capable, or prestigious we may be. "Location," as the realtors say, determines value and price, and these measures are related to the prestige bestowed upon the one who lives in such a location. We try to acquire those things which bring with them prestige and respect. We can then take pride in having them.

If we are fortunate enough to attend a college or university, the particular one it is carries with it a whole set of feelings about prestige and the pride we may or may not take in being affiliated with that institution. Harvard has a different level of prestige than the University of Miami, even though both are excellent institutions of learning. Indeed, it seems at times that many parents are more concerned with the level of prestige a school has rather than the kind of education their child may receive. Much is invested in SE for parent and child regarding the name of the institution. This name, like clothing, home, street, and automobile, will determine to some extent how each feels individually, with the SE Switch telling them it is a good

70

or a bad thing. One can almost smell the reaction some people have when told the name of a college another person is attending. Like the animal world of pecking orders, there exists a prestige hierarchy of institutions of higher learning. SE Switches on both sides of the conversation are eager to play the game.

I have used the words self-esteem, pride, prestige, power, and respect in reference to the topics discussed. Other words in the same family are reputation, worthiness, deserving, image, character, and integrity. Words which relate to harm or injury to what these concepts represent are insulting, demeaning, offensive, attacking, scornful, contemptuous, abusive, and disdainful.

A word like "pride," most commonly used in relation to accomplishment of some type, either by an individual or by someone close to the individual, reflects one of the most pleasurable of kinds of sensations we can experience. The feelings associated with the pride of completing a marathon, or graduating from college, or helping someone in need are profoundly satisfying. The feelings or pride a parent has in watching a child learn to ride a bike or perform well in a school play, or get the winning hit in a baseball game, are of a similar nature, perhaps even richer in positive emotional content. Those feelings which cause people to use the expression, "that's what it is all about," are so wonderful and uplifting, there are not easily found words to describe them, because they seem to get at that root feeling of what is best about being alive. It is a kind of euphoria that attends these feelings of pride.

Prestige is something we bestow on another if we have been convinced the person has enough attributes to deserve our respect. There are of course unlimited degrees of prestige, and the person with the prestige may have the same, more, or less than we have either in general or relating to a specific area of life. The person with the prestige usually knows it exists and takes some pleasure from feeling engendered by the granting of that prestige. Like pride, feelings of prestige are extremely satisfying and pleasant. While there may not be euphoria, there is a definite sense of well-being and satisfaction attendant to having prestige. Of course, with the prestige usually comes a sense of power, worthiness, and deserving, which also have wonderfully positive emotional tones accompanying them. The effect produced in such individuals is an experience of deep comfort and satisfaction.

Pride and prestige, I believe, come from those old neural or brain mechanisms I call the SE Switch. This probable limbic lobe device has taken what was a survival signal to more primitive mammals, and brought it along into our human brains, creating what are some of the most common and universally experienced emotions considered part of our human nature. They indeed are so integral to what we do every day so as almost to be taken for granted. Like getting up in the morning and going to sleep at night, we tend not to question what really is going on in the brain when these feelings are experienced. The feelings are so common, we have not needed to look at them critically. Perhaps, as already noted regarding the concept of natural selection, which eluded thinkers for many years, there is something about our human nature keeping us from looking at the most basic things about ourselves. The most interesting thing about pride and prestige is not so much whether someone has lots or little, but rather that the notion exists at all.

When we are insulted, demeaned, or scorned, our pride and prestige are threatened and we do not like it. Depending on our state of mind, the issues at stake, and who is leveling the insult, most of us will feel badly. As pleasant as the positive feelings were when we experience pride and prestige, those emotions we experience when those attributes are attacked can be awful. Depending on the persons involved, the feelings may be so unpleasant as to require some sudden and dramatic action, like what occurred with Admiral Inman. More commonly, there may simply be hurt, pain, or sadness, and this may turn into anger, hatred, or the desire to harm the perpetrator.

In Admiral Inman's case, even though he enjoyed high prestige from his prior accomplishments, and presumably enjoyed the pleasant feelings of pride associated with that prestige, when his integrity was questioned, as it often is in Senate confirmation hearings, he found it intolerable to remain in that arena. The pain of what he perceived as insults to him was so great he needed to defuse the sensation. He did so by lashing out against his critics and by going home. The unusual aspect of this behavior was that an experienced career government official does not usually have such "thin skin." People in the public area tend to withstand criticism more easily than others, perhaps a requisite for a successful public figure. We can only speculate what caused the Admiral to react the way he did, but I believe the root cause was the magnitude of the pain felt when he perceived his prestige and integrity were being questioned.

I think the SE Switch was the culprit. It probably served him well in terms of the beneficial and pleasant feelings associated with positive signals sent by it, but in this circumstance the SE Switch likely caused him to withdraw inappropriately, something I believe happens to all of us at times. I think Admiral Inman was defeated by the messages sent by the SE Switch. Since by all other measures, he was capable of being an effective Secretary of Defense, having a fine resumé for that position, we can only conclude that some very strong emotions got in the way. The SE Switch evolved to send unmistakable emotional messages to its owner, creating a situation demanding some kind of action.

In our introductory example of sumo wrestling, an American-born man of Japanese heritage has captured the Japanese national title of sumo wrestling. National pride and prestige are exhibited everyday in the same way such phenomena occur with individuals. Diplomacy, negotiation, competition, conflict, aggression, and war are some of the ways nations deal with one another. All these methods utilize measurements of degrees of pride, prestige, and power. National pride can cause a nation to rise to heroism in the face of aggression by stronger nations, or it can lead a nation to become an aggressor because it feels entitled or worthy to gain control of or dominate and rule another nation or territory. History is replete with such examples. While I do not mean to imply that the main thing motivating nations to act or react in a particular way has only to do with pride and prestige, I do suggest those things exist as powerful forces at the national level, as well as the individual level. It seems clear those forces also exist at the neighborhood, community, city, and state levels, as well as in educational institutions. Pride and prestige are facets of almost every kind of organized group, be it at the most local level, like a cub scout pack, or a think tank, or within a country or government.

But to get back to the example, an unusual phenomenon occurred which seemed to alter the normal operation of the pride and prestige emotions. Because the sumo champion was raised in the U.S., the Japanese were confounded about how to react or feel about his victory. Here was a custom of long tradition in Japan being dominated by an American born of Japanese parents. The Japanese authorities did not know whether to grant him the award. Their SE Switches were probably either frozen in neutral or more likely vacillating to positive and negative with strong emotions connected to each polarity. Should they celebrate this wonderful tradition freely, or should they minimize it because an American won? If your parents are Japanese,

74

and you look Japanese but were born and raised in another country, are you Japanese? Are you entitled to be included as a member of that group, and should you be treated with the respect a member of that group would ordinarily enjoy if there was nothing ambiguous about his membership? Isn't it enough that you look like a Japanese sumo wrestler, compete in Japan against the very best, and ultimately win the contest?

The answer to that question was no. The Japanese officials denied the award. Being raised in the U.S. created an ambiguity in feelings as to "who" prevailed in the competition. Did the U.S. win, or did Japan win? This was not intended to be an international competition. Was the winner American or Japanese? Eventually, the officials did award the honor to the victor. Their SE Switches were stymied: create feelings of jubilation, as it ordinarily does with a great victory, or send the "I'm not so good message," the result of a perceived or real defeat. From the lack of publicity in this country, it appeared the U.S.'s collective SE Switch also was confounded. Rather than exhibit expressions of pride and accomplishment, those aware of the outcome behaved in a matter of fact way, compared to an Olympic victory, where there would be great jubilation and celebration. Was he really an American?

How individual's SE Switches on each side of the Pacific were affected by this event determined how much individual pride and prestige were attached, and this in turn decided how much national pride and prestige were exhibited. The ancient SE Switch designed to assist in survival and to avoid errors in judgment, became sabotaged by ambiguity. In this example, the reality of modern society confronted some old customs, and confusion reigned. Was the sumo champion an exalted member of an elite group, or an outsider who threatened a long-established and cherished practice of a proud people? The SE Switch was stymied, no clear emotional signals were sent, and the resulting actions were confused and inconsistent.

In 1997, on the upper west side in N.Y.C., a 31-year-old high school teacher named Jonathan Levin was murdered in his apartment. Mr. Levin had come from an extremely wealthy family and did not need to work for a living. He had chosen teaching as a career, selecting the inner city and its disadvantaged students as the group to whom he would devote his attentions. In a short time, he became admired by his colleagues and students for his talents, energy, and devotion to work. He developed a fine reputation and earned much prestige. Jonathan Levin was respectful of his students, going out of his way to encourage them in their studies and also in their personal lives. He recognized how important the creation of improved SE in his students was to their development and future success or failure in life.

The 19-year-old who murdered him had been one of his students. He had been expelled from high school, had no job and no realistic plans for the future. No evidence existed that Mr. Levin had done any harm to him. Very shortly after the crime, he boasted to his friends about what he had done.

In an Op-ED piece in *The New York Times* on June 16, 1997, Bob Herbert wrote about this crime from the vantage point of respect. He pointed out that Mr. Levin clearly had developed an "exalted status," and enjoyed considerable respect. Herbert postulated that Mr. Arthur, the alleged murderer, received no respect, and this was his motive, namely to destroy someone of high prestige, and by doing so attain respect and admiration from his peers. He wrote:

> "In the world inhabited by Corey Arthur, there is an extraordinary number of hapless individuals, mostly male, whom roam the streets and ride the subways raging at their insignificance, at their isolation and

chronic inability to deal successfully with the larger world, at the contempt and disdain with which they are viewed by so many, including themselves. They are obsessed with gaining respect. Unable to achieve it in more conventional ways they turn to violence."

The unpleasant feelings which accompany signals of low SE most often cause withdrawal and lack of aggression. Absence of pride and prestige in an individual, depending on other things occurring in his life at the moment, may express themselves in many ways. If Mr. Herbert is correct, and I believe he is, Mr. Arthur would destroy a person known to him and his peers with high prestige and respect in order to gain some for himself. The irony being, this was what Mr. Levin tried to create for his students, not take from them. His mere existence as a symbol of success, however, must have overcome whatever feelings of gratitude Mr. Arthur might have developed towards his teacher. There is always some potential for resentment towards those who help us, because that help defines a scenario which has someone who needs some help, and therefore is less capable or powerful in at least a particular circumstance. Being helped may evoke feelings of anger towards the helper. This should not surprise those who have tried to teach a spouse something, help a teenage child, or a senior citizen who does not seem to think any help is needed. Each of those people is quickly capable of expressing anger towards the helper. *This is because of feelings experienced when the SE Switch reacted to the individual's inability to perform the task, sending messages with unpleasant content which eventuated in anger.* A later chapter will discuss this phenomenon in greater detail.

Russell Baker on June 4, 1997 in his Observer column in *The New York Times* also wrote about anger and respect in an article entitled "Gunning for Respect." He pondered the origin of the idea that death or maiming is the just punishment for disrespectful people. Manifestations of such disrespect now include: looking someone in the eye, bumping into him on sidewalks or public conveyences, and driving a car in a manner unacceptable to him. In trying to understand the crave for respect, he wondered if the easy availability of guns or the urge to humble the insolent and powerful, comprised the root cause of casual slaughter. Baker talked about the well known "pleasure in revenge when giving someone his comeupance, and watching your victim realize how completely he underestimated you." He understood some of the forces operating when violence is involved in attempting to gain respect.

The articles by Herbert and Baker, seemed to be searching for better explanations for what provokes enough anger in someone to unleash brutality and even murder in situations where no real offense had been committed. I think this behavior must be at least partly related to those feelings which surround the violent individual's perceptions of his own pride, prestige, SE, and what, as noted earlier, biologists have called "resource holding potential." As we have seen, those human conceptualizations stem from the internal biological signals and emotions our brains produce as they evaluate and review for us "how we are doing." If someone's brain, in the evaluative mechanism I call the SE Switch, develops intolerably unpleasant sensations which are persistent, they will probably do something to get rid of those feelings. What they choose is based on many factors, including intelligence, educational level, maturity, emotional stability, peer pressure, impulsivity, the magnitude of the SE Switch's negative messages, and their ability to deal with those unpleasant sensations. If the emotional signals are overwhelming, drastic action may ensue.

Healthy people usually choose mechanisms which are not overtly hurtful to others, like accomplishing some goal in an unrelated area to achieve recognition or, like our FBI employee, finding fault in someone else, but in a gentle way. One might also, like the Admiral, simply get out of the kitchen, leave the arena which is creating the pain. One might become charitable and help others, one might seek refuge in a new religion or practice, or maybe even write a book.

But some people, because the pain is so great, and because they feel desperate and angry, turn to violence to seek removal of the pain, and at least temporarily gain some satisfaction related to improved SE and the prestige which might go with it, even if in the end they know it will ultimately lead to their own destruction.

On the lighter side, but still demonstrative of how perceived offenses against one's prestige can create some interesting behavior, are the following examples:

In April, 1998, during an NBA playoff game between the N.Y. Knicks and Miami Heat, Larry Johnson of the Knicks verbally taunted Alonzo Mourning of the Heat, saying some insulting things, trying to provoke him into an error or fit of anger. Mourning, familiar with this kind of strategy, fell for it anyway, took a swing at Johnson, was suspended for the next game which the Knicks won easily, eliminating the Heat from the playoffs. Mourning, when asked why he reacted the way he did, said, "I had to defend my manhood." The Heat's fate was sealed by their player's inability to ward off the negative feelings from an SE Switch flipped by an insult. Mourning could not tolerate the feelings associated with his perception that his prestige had been injured by his competitor. One does not need to be a scientist to understand the power of the SE Switch. He may simply need to know how to activate it to achieve his purpose.

A prominent divorce attorney who perceives that opposing counsel and his client do not pay her enough respect by responding to her threats without fear, becomes angry and complicates litigation with unnecessary motions and legal tactics. In doing so, she makes major errors on behalf of her client because she had been blinded by the anger of the feelings produced by her SE Switch. Her self-judged prestige, and all the power and entitlements which ordinarily went with it, were in her mind under threat, producing an intolerable set of feelings. Instead of helping her client, she hurt her. Lawyers should learn more about the SE Switch.

There is virtually no limit to the examples one could choose to dramatize further the amazing effects of our brain's evaluation of how we are being treated and how it thinks we are doing. Other dramatic examples appear in the news everyday: like the Speaker of the House choosing to close down government offices because he was not treated respectfully regarding seating on Air Force One; the ballplayer leaving a multimillion-dollar-a-year job because he feels he has not been paid enough respect; a network morning show star who leaves the program because the female co-anchor appears to get more credit for the show's success than he does. One could catalogue dozens of events where, because of some event relating to pride or prestige, someone has had a strong emotional message sent by his SE Switch which reacts as if he were in great danger, rather than simply alive in the 21st century.

Chapter 7

"Being Right"

*"We believe, first and foremost, what makes us feel
that we are fine fellows."*

Bertrand Russell, 1950

This chapter is the most important in the book, because our need to be "right" is one of the most basic and influential parts of our human nature. From the simplest act, like putting one foot in front of the other while walking, to the very complex act of solving a difficult engineering problem, we have a practical need to be "right," namely not to walk off a cliff, and not to construct a building that might collapse. More importantly, we have an emotional reason to be "right."

It is not difficult to understand why the evolutionary process would produce mechanisms to allow us to perform an act without that act also killing us. Our five senses do many things, but the most basic thing they do is help keep us alive. By being able to smell, see, hear, touch, and taste we can do things which are relatively safe. The process of natural selection has tossed out traits which did not work so well, and has kept the ones which have. Remember that to pass on a trait to your offspring, you must have survived to do it. The traits we have, by definition, were of such

81

nature that they allowed our ancestors to live and survive, and eventually to beget us.

Our species has evolved with sophisticated equipment generally keeping it out of trouble and permitting it to stay alive. We trust our senses to accomplish these goals either because confidence in our senses is built into us via the evolutionary process or, through trial and error, we have learned to rely on their messages. By using the equipment we have, we tend to know what is dangerous and what is safe. Some of the hardware we have, in addition to providing us with direct sensory information, also produces feelings or emotions. Certain smells, sights, sounds, touches, and tastes are associated with profound emotional experience. These emotions help guide us. The evolutionary process has seen fit to construct our brains so associations of emotion are attached to the primary senses, providing additional information to help us make the best choices and decisions. Evolution's "genius," in integrating existing structures and functions with the newer equipment of emotional experience, produced higher quality information for our needs. Some of the emotions which evolved are: fear, pleasure, aversion, attraction, happiness, sadness, confidence, and insecurity. Emotional tones of feeling accompany almost every experience we have. They may be steady and consistent, or change rapidly as circumstances change. They may be subtle or dramatic. When profound, these emotions tend to provoke us into some action, like running away, having sex, looking away, looking towards, smiling, crying, being assertive, or being quiet.

The emotional connections to "being right" or "being wrong" can be as dramatic as those attached to our sensory perceptions and, on an evolutionary basis, have developed to assist us in succeeding and surviving in the world. Because of the kinds of creatures we are, and the kind of civilization we reside in, behavior having to do with "being right" and not "wrong" is among the most common behavior we all exhibit. It is this phenomenon which the rest of this chapter is devoted to, the emotional message sent by the SE Switch relating to "being right."

While I recognize that much of what I will talk about here is of a complex nature, as described in the Introduction, I have again relied on the Occam's Razor approach to analyze difficult and complicated issues, namely that the simplest explanation is most often the right one.

Why are most young students so eager to raise their hands in class and give the teacher the correct answer to a question? Their enthusiasm is reminiscent of the screaming fans rooting for their team in a local sporting event. Why are they motivated to demonstrate they know the answer? In thinking about this scenario, one can of course imagine many reasons this would be so, like simply wanting to please the teacher, or responding to what has been asked of them. But, as with the other examples previously noted, there is a strong emotional force compelling the young student to behave in a certain way. The drive is to demonstrate to the teacher, classmates, and perhaps himself that he knows the correct answer. Whatever our academic backgrounds, as children we probably all have had the experience of being confident we knew the answer to a question posed in class, and feeling excited and enthusiastic about the possibility of being called upon to offer it. That excitement could quickly turn into euphoria if we were indeed selected and provided the correct answer. It might be particularly satisfying and pleasant if others in the class had given the wrong answer, and we gave the correct one.

What's the big deal? Why should such a simple act be full of so much emotion? Did so much really depend on the demonstration of our knowledge, rather than just quietly realizing we knew the answer? Probably not. In the grand scheme of things, knowing or not knowing an answer to a particular question should not necessarily have much significance attached to it. But, as previously mentioned, if one is walking in a dangerous area, it is better to be right about where the next step should be taken to avoid the danger. Thinking that $3\times4=13$ can create problems for us. It will lead us into a situation which is probably not advantageous. So, logically, it is simply better to know the correct answer than the incorrect one. But why should knowing that $3\times4=12$ create so much positive emotion within the students [us]? I suspect this phenomenon has to do with evolution's blind but brilliant "plan" to give us strong emotional signals as guideposts to when we are right and when we are wrong.

We have been designed to feel great when we are right. We have been designed to feel not so great when wrong. These emotions evolved to enable us to make choices, to know what course to take, which direction to go in, and to help guarantee our success in any undertaking requiring correct decisions.

These emotions also become ends in themselves because we learn quickly how good it feels to be right, and so we tend to pursue activities, like showing the teacher and classmates that we know the answer, to get that wonderful payoff of euphoria which comes with "being right." Not only is there personal satisfaction accompanying the knowledge of knowing the answer, but there is a powerful set of forces unleashed which have to do with the pleasures associated with the recognition of "being right." These are not easily forgotten and almost demand to be experienced again.

I am suggesting that evolution has produced within our brains, probably within the limbic system, a mechanism which I call the SE Switch, which rewards us with strongly positive kinds of emotion when we get something right. This very pleasant sensation may also become the object of certain activities pursued by the individual in order to turn the SE Switch on so he can then experience the feelings. The student raises his hand because by knowing the answer he is already experiencing the positive emotions which assist him in venturing forth, but also because he knows how good it is going to feel when he is recognized as having given the correct answer to his teacher.

Our brains and minds devote tremendous amounts of time and energy to activities related to being right. So much of what we see everyday in our own personal interactions with people and of those who are prominent enough to come to our attention in various kinds of media has to do with the need for people to be right.

In the workplace, much of the interaction of people at every level has to do with each one's need to be right, a dynamic often leading to tension, and certainly at times to positive and negative emotions. Proposals by staff members of an organization about how to proceed on a particular issue are usually competing and filled with strong individual proprietary feelings and senses of correctness. The issue may be as simple as what temperature to keep the thermostat in the office, or as complex as developing a long term strategic plan for a company. Regardless of the seriousness of the issue, the dynamics are the same in each example. Individuals formulate an opinion, and then compete with others who have different opinions. Each comes from a place of inwardly feeling right about the issue, however they have arrived at that opinion. Each will argue, probably fervently, on behalf of his belief. All hope the person or persons with the power to make the decision will agree with them. The person whose plan is chosen will enjoy the positive emotions generated by the SE Switch from having been recognized or validated as having been right. The individuals who lose will experience those unpleasant sensations which occur when one is wrong. They will dislike the feeling and then probably do something in an effort to defuse it, most likely attempting to convince others their idea *really was better,* even though a final decision had already been made.

The fruits or droppings of evolution are as evident at the water cooler as in the bedroom or Supreme Court. We will go to great lengths to demonstrate that we are right. Almost all arguments we have are about this at some level. Marital spats, often about a trivial issue, may take on major emotional overtones because each participant needs to be right. Sibling squabbles are highly partisan and the participants usually present their cases to the parent with tremendous amounts of emotion. Friendships are often tested by incidents where each individual has his own read on an event, feeling he is right and his friend wrong, the need to be right or validated sometimes surpassing the need to preserve the friendship. Members of Congress may argue a point, as in the impeachment trial of President Clinton, determined that they are right, on the moral high ground, on the right side of history, but behave so self-righteously, they actually do harm to all they purportedly hold dear, including their previously excellent reputations.

The emotional benefit in "being right" drives the individual to succeed in his quest to be right. It feels good to know you are right, and it feels even better when you can convince others that you are. This is a powerful elixir. So powerful that the drive often seems more important than the actual outcome of an argument. We spend considerable amounts of time arguing with spouses, family, and friends about issues whose outcome would probably not change our lives dramatically one way or another. And yet the passions involved in arguing the various sides of the cases are strong. Why should there be such passion?

I believe the answer lies in our evolved equipment. We become impassioned about "being right," not so much because a particular issue is weighty, but because it is in our natures to be that way. Our limbic systems make us that way. We are imbued with emotions helping us to know if we are right, and feelings making it important to actually be right. The feelings are the main drivers. No matter how intellectually driven we are, those feelings are the engines powering much of what we do. David Hume, the British philosopher, proposed "the intellect is the slave of the passions." We can offer rational explanations for our behavior but it often is governed more by how we feel, rather than what we think.

Why are people defensive? We see evidence and reference to it all the time. When someone is criticized, even the most enlightened among us tend at first to defend the action being questioned. Even if we recognize the validity of the complaint and have the maturity to react to the criticism in a positive way, something in us wants to rationalize or justify the action. When criticism is clearly invalid, we may react with tremendous emotion, usually indignation, and people who witness this call us sensitive or defensive.

Why, if the criticism is unjust, should it call up so much emotion? Why not just laugh, since we know it is not a correct judgment? Perhaps Buddha or the Dalai Lama could, but most of us would have feelings we did not like, and could not laugh. Even veteran psychiatrists can react with indignation when they have been criticized in a way they perceive is unfair or inaccurate. I believe we react this way because the criticism goes directly to the SE Switch for processing. It evaluates whether we are right or wrong. If the SE Switch receives information telling us we may be wrong when we thought we were right, it sends our negative, unpleasant emotional signals to our awareness alerting us to proceed with caution.

Criticism challenges the comfort we felt in believing we were right about something. This outside criticism is a thunderbolt to our limbic system, which is monitoring how we are doing and sending us appropriate emotional signals to let us know how we are doing. Our limbic system thought we were OK one moment, but was jarred in the next. It reacts to this unanticipated challenge with powerful feelings, as if our existence were being threatened, not just our opinion, because that is what it was designed to do.

It does not necessarily matter how important the issue is. It only matters how the limbic system reacts. Because of our own unique genetic makeups, our individual life experiences, our particular baggage, and our coloration of perceptions, we each may react somewhat differently in terms of the magnitude and quality of the response. But I believe we all basically have the same type of reaction, namely not to like how it feels, and probably to take some action to defend ourselves. What this most commonly is manifested by is defensive argument with the person bringing the criticism. Or we may mount a counter-criticism in an attempt to manipulate the other person into retracting his criticism of us. Of course, those strategies rarely work. Neither will the criticizer remove the criticism, nor will the counterattack defuse the feelings generated by the SE Switch. Such counter-criticisms are usually counterproductive, as any corporate human resources person or psychotherapist would note.

Defensiveness is just a short stop away from jealousy, perhaps engendered by it at times. A more subtle form of criticism is embraced in those encounters where someone puts forth a new idea in a field or organization which others wish they had thought of first. Jealousy is a feeling relating to not having something which someone else has. If that "thing" is owning a new idea, this can be felt as a criticism in that the new idea confronts someone else's sense of "being right." As with direct criticism, the individual who feels threatened may go on the attack, even when the new idea does not really damage them in any measurable way. The same dynamic operates, namely the SE Switch recognizes a threat to being right, and sends unpleasant messages causing the individual to take action to defuse the feeling. He may then counterattack the individual who had the idea. Such attacks represent a common kind of behavior among many academicians in various fields.

In the field of Sociobiology, many distinguished evolutionary scientists have felt more comfortable attacking new ideas, even misrepresenting them, because those ideas were not their own. They reacted in the same way as if *they* had been criticized, their own sense of "being right" suddenly threatened, sending unacceptable messages from their limbic lobes telling them they were under siege, and creating those unpleasant feelings which often lead to defensive behaviors.

Could lying be a similar phenomenon? Experts say all of us lie at some time There are of course many circumstances where a lie is the moral thing to do; for example, protecting the life of a loved one in danger, or protecting someone's feelings other than one's own. But there are many situations when we lie about ourselves strictly to protect our emotions and perhaps our prestige. If a question answered honestly would make us look "wrong" compared to what we have put out in the world as looking "right," limbic system arousal may provoke us to lie rather than feel those negative emotions associated with suddenly being wrong. For example, if we have convinced ourselves that some questionable action we have taken is really O.K., and we have become emotionally comfortable with the choice, our limbic system is relatively comfortable. But, if challenged, and the true answer to a question would make it appear that what we had done was not O.K., then we might lie. We lie to feel better about ourselves. Like being defensive, we may lie to protect against those awful feelings which accompany "being wrong," as well as to simply avoid the practical aspects of standing corrected.

From our adversarial legal system to playing Trivial Pursuit, we love to be right and hate to be wrong.

A tradition in the medical profession is honoring those physicians who are right. Training of physicians all too often includes aspects of "one upsmanship," behaviors more designed to demonstrate who really "knows the answer" rather than pure teaching and learning. In medical training centers, there is often a continuing game played among house staff and attending physicians as to who is the best at getting it right, who knows the best answer or the best method for something, issues pertaining more to emotionally driven activity than what may be best for the patient or for education. Fortunately, this kind of constant stimulation of the SE Switch usually ends up being good for the patient because it often produces the best diagnosis and treatment. "Being right" is usually a good thing.

Members of the legal profession often seem to have a great share of the self righteousness market. They argue in our adversarial system as if there is only one way to view a dispute. Of course, this is how the system is designed to operate, that full partisan representations of events will eventually produce the truth. What seems to occur all too often, however, to the detriment of those who hire a lawyer, is that each opposing attorney gets trapped in the "being right" battle mode, making chances for settlement or solution to the problem more remote. The emotional need to be right, to prevail, to have it your way drives the case more than the specific issues at stake. The system is set up for the lawyers to act on their basic needs to be right. Not only is this system designed to be adversarial to start with, the lawyers are also paid to the adversarial. Those SE Switches are pushed into the fast forward mode in the direction of confidence, hubris, and aggression and the lawyers feel very good about what they are doing. No wonder attempts to utilize arbitration rather than litigation are talked about as a better way to settle many legal matters.

Self righteous people tend to be very sure they are right about their opinions and judgments. It seems hard for them to see the other side of an argument. They are always right. It is not a stretch to speculate that the main reason for this may be how uncomfortable they feel when challenged with alternative views. Once they have taken a position, they rarely budge. One explanation for their rigidity is that the feelings experienced, if their "righteousness" were in jeopardy, were so unpleasantly powerful, they needed to find a psychological defense mechanism to ward off the pain of "being wrong." In the past, they may have experienced such discomfort when being criticized, and learned simply not to be receptive to or to process ideas counter to their own belief systems. They have found a way to disarm the SE Switch. For them, it no longer reacts violently to challenge about whether the correct path has been chosen. The SE Switch has been dampened or quieted to allow their sense of what is right to prevail without the fear of activation. We have all known people like this. Many politicians have become experts in this field of always "being right," although their SE Switches may be fully operational when reviewing other kinds of events and activities.

"Talking head" political T.V. shows have become popular. There seems to be a great attraction to watching experts express their views about current issues and events. Some of these shows have formats encouraging aggressive kinds of displays in voicing one's opinion. Some thrive on it, namely the full expression of the guest's position, not only putting forth his own arguments but actually attacking those positions of the other guests. It is not just a debate of ideas but a vitriolic contest. One would guess there is some pleasure taken by the guest who is in the attack mode. One might also guess that the regular viewers are also taking pleasure watching the attacks. On these shows, nothing is decided which will change any viewer's life in any material way. Yet, there is some obvious attraction watching a guest go on the attack about opinions closely held by the viewer. In my opinion, the "attack guest," and the viewer identifying with him, both enjoy those feelings and emotions that go along with "being right." It seems immensely pleasurable for the participants to compete in these contests, and I believe it is the emotional payoff connected to "being right" which drives the talking head and watcher to become so involved.

Predictions made by expert guests also fall into this domain of "the need to be right." Whether in politics, law, finance, or sport, a whole culture has grown up related to predicting what is going to happen. Even when the O.J. jury verdict or the Senate impeachment trial verdicts were only moments away, the experts had been lined up and the T.V. shows were poised to ask how it would turn out. What possible benefit could there be to knowing this information a few moments before the real event would take place, other than to demonstrate who was right?

The drive to show that one's opinion is correct is enormous. The respect gained if one was correct is substantial. The pre-game sports analysts appear genuinely eager to hawk their opinions. They are more likely driven by some other force wanting them to be right. Expert legal minds, like Alan Dershowitz, when seen on T.V., are passionate well beyond their desire to promote themselves. They really have strong emotions attached to the positions they take on the talk shows, even when those positions have nothing to do with the outcome of a case. Stock market predictors argue with great conviction about their ideas. In these cases, if proven right, benefits, beyond the simple firing of their SE Switches, will accrue to them.

From men needing to be unassisted in determining routes on auto trips, to a policeman's self satisfaction in citing a motorist for a "moving violation," we are all involved in activities which contain the seeds of issues which have something to do with "being right." We all do it. It usually happens on an unconscious level but it drives us forcefully. While we can intellectualize or find practical justifications for what we do, many times the more basic reason is we simply have the emotional need to be right. This need is part of our human nature. The evolutionary process has put it there. It has helped us survive. The mechanism designed to prevent us from making dangerous errors now also serves a different function. The means has become an end in itself. We love to be right because it feels good. We hate to be wrong because it feels bad.

Chapter 8

SE Impairment

"Is not man himself the most unsettled of all the creatures of the Earth? What is this trembling sensation that is intensified with each ascending step in the natural order?"

Ugo Betti, 1953

We probably all know people who seem to have little confidence. They may be fearful about most of the things which confront them in life, and they tend to underestimate their assets, from their physical appearance to their intellectual or social capabilities. Somehow they manage to get through, but with not much ambition or pleasure. People around them often feel those folks have more to offer than they themselves realize, and may try to help by encouraging them to feel better about themselves. These people, even if motivated to get help, are challenges for any therapist. Unless they are depressed or have some specific past event at the root of these feelings, it is hard to change how they feel.

Most of us have reasonable amounts of confidence in our abilities to get things done or to compete at something. These feelings of confidence or our assessment of our SE may vary from day to day but are generally consistent over the long haul. We may become more or less confident in a particular area as time goes on based on our accomplishments or failures, but if we are normal, our basic approach to life remains pretty constant. We generally have a reasonably clear picture in our minds of our capabilities and also tend to know what we are not so good at. Many of us seem, with age, to become more comfortable with whatever limitations we believe we have, becoming more accepting of ourselves. We may, however, always remain terribly fearful of certain situations, no matter how much we have matured, public speaking being high on the list.

Psychiatrists, psychologists, and psychiatric social workers work with patients with many kinds of mental disorders. A very common symptom they confront, which may often be part of another clinical condition, is the complaint that the patient does not measure up to others, that he or she is just not good enough. These patients often have pervasive feelings of inadequacy, and these emotions can be unpleasant and sometimes even devastating. Such feelings may even have a sickening quality associated with them, and because of the miserable nature of the sensations, they may drive the patient having them to do something to attempt to minimize them. Some people withdraw socially, protecting themselves from interactions with others, which may actually make them feel worse about themselves. Others may be on a constant quest to engage in activities they hope will make them feel better about themselves. Neither strategy works because their underlying belief remains that they just are not worthy, that they do not make the grade. They tend to remain chronically unhappy.

Therapists working with these patients look at their life events, especially in childhood, searching for circumstances which might have contributed to the individual having feelings of low SE. Their strategy is based on the notion if a patient can understand what forces were acting on him, which might have done injury to his SE, then he may be able to overcome those feelings. Clearly this kind of therapy has merit, for there often are wrongs done to us, most often by our parents. We may not have understood well enough the impact those wrongs have had in determining how we see ourselves as adults. Any time we can see reasons why we feel the way we do, it may make us feel somewhat better. Therapy, and the intellectual understanding which comes from it, can help a patient see things which may have been injurious to his SE. And, as this book has been suggesting, because of our evolutionary endowment and the extreme emotional penalty we pay for "being wrong," placing "blame" in another place may help us feel better about ourselves. We can, as will be suggested later, find ways to outwit the SE Switch.

But maybe, for many people, their low sense of SE is simply the way they came, not related necessarily to any known medical or psychiatric disorder, but because there is something wrong with their SE Switches. Perhaps for some people, the SE Switch does not work the way it does for "normal" people. There are many examples in human physiology of genetically determined disorders of regulation of various mechanisms in the body. An example is that some people secrete more stomach acid than others, usually creating some symptoms. In these people, this tendency has nothing to do with parental upbringing but is the result of factors genetically determined which cause the lining cells of the stomach to make more acid than is necessary to do the job. There are dozens of other examples of disorders in humans, where internally regulated feedback mechanisms, controlling things from thyroid hormone levels to heart rate and blood pressure levels, are out of whack, creating clinical symptoms and diseases. In these examples, the normal regulatory mechanisms which keep things in balance are deranged. This may occur because certain signals are misread, or the receiving devices or receptors are too insensitive to the signals sent, or the receptors overreact to the signals received. The result is the secretion of too much of a hormone or the generation of an exaggerated electrical message in the central nervous system.

If there is something akin to an SE Switch within us, scientifically speaking, it takes no great leap of faith to assume that in some people, the SE Switch may simply be defective. If it works like other mechanisms in the body, then it has to receive information from some other place in the body, process that information, and then react to it in some way sending out signals or messages to another part of the body. Problems may occur anywhere along this pathway. Like a light bulb which suddenly will not light, there may be a defect with the line carrying the incoming power, or a faulty light fixture, or the bulb itself may be broken or burned out. The same kinds of problems occur in the human body. Medical doctors, like electricians, are trained to track down the location of the problem, and also if possible to determine what caused the problem as well as, of course, trying to repair it.

One could imagine situations where a SE Switch did not receive proper incoming information. This could be due to problems with the various sensory organs, or along the electrical, circulatory, or hormonal pathways connecting the sensory organs to that part of the limbic lobe in the brain where the SE Switch is postulated to be. There could be something wrong with the SE Switch itself, where it receives proper and pertinent information, but simply is malfunctioning and not able to process the information, or there may be a problem in pathways leading from the SE Switch, so that normal signals never arrive suitably at their intended destinations.

In people who seem to have inexplicably low SE, perhaps it is not so much how they were raised, but rather something wrong with the mechanisms relating to limbic lobe function. Perhaps their SE Switches simply favor sending inappropriate signals to their consciousness which make them feel unworthy. Perhaps the SE Switch is sending the wrong information.

Remember, the basic assumption about the SE Switch is that it was an evolutionary mechanism which helped animals make correct choices. It would serve the animal by sending emotional messages to tell it to feel confident and move ahead, or to withdraw and be cautious. If the SE Switch was defective, and sent emotional signals to withdraw, when it would have been more appropriate for the animal to persist and be confident, then the animal would be handicapped. If this happened to humans, it could create a chronic situation where the individual was impaired. Rather than the existence of some dark, psychological secret of abuse in the past, maybe the SE Switch is just faulty. Some of us may be incredibly well coordinated physically, some not. Some of us may have normal SE Switches, some may not. A fouled SE Switch could result because of genetic factors, accidents in embryology where the SE Switch does not form properly as the fetal body is developing, birth injuries, results of hidden infection, and so on.

A more common situation than people who always have low SE is when a particular event creates inappropriately severe feelings of low SE. The examples of this kind of experience are legion. The golfer who hits the bad shot and who reacts with tremendous emotion, wanting to throw his club, is experiencing intense feelings of low SE. He often will overtly say disparaging things about himself in response to feelings he is experiencing. It may take quite awhile for the feelings to settle down and for him to regain his composure. The student who, when called upon, either does not know the answer to a question or who provides the wrong answer, may suffer waves of humiliation and low SE which take some time to dissipate. The customer who is disrespectfully treated by the salesperson may experience feelings of rage, as might the driver whose right of way is ignored by another motorist, these feelings dissolving only very slowly. Could these situations, where we react more strongly and emotionally than even we think we should, be related to something beyond our upbringing, education, life experience, and maturity? Could it simply be that our SE Switches overreact? That they respond disproportionately to the event, flooding us with negative emotion.

If the SE Switch is there, judging and evaluating what is going before us, helping us to evaluate the world in front of us and our performance in it, it would seem logical that at times, based on many different factors, the SE Switch simply may send out signals which are too strong relative to the event which took place. So what in reality is just a simple failure, a transient, unimportant glitch in our overall well being, gets transformed into a raging cauldron of emotion. Is a missed 3-foot putt in golf really so awful? To golfers, it certainly feels that way sometimes, the self loathing and agony of the failure occurring as if a serious life event had befallen them. Is not being treated respectfully by a salesperson really so bad? If a driver is discourteous to us, as long as our life was not jeopardized, should we feel so angry? Perhaps the SE Switch is just too active in these circumstances, simply overreacting to the implied threat to our sense of how capable, prestigious, or important we are. Maybe we are no more self-important than the next person, but that our SE Switches, not necessarily designed for modern day activities, just overshoots sending messages which make us feel badly. Remember, the equipment we have has come along over millions of years, well before there was golf, department stores, and automobiles.

Most people suffering from depression have feelings of low SE as part of the syndrome. People who have bipolar disorder will vary from feeling poorly about themselves to feeling outrageously upbeat. Patients with so called borderline personality may vary in idealization and reverence for an individual with sudden hatred and rage against the same individual if they perceive not enough attention or respect has been paid them. Could some of these people have disordered SE Switch mechanisms as part of their disease?

Most experts believe that patients who suffer from alcohol or drug dependency are different from normal people in some way, which makes it harder for them to avoid excess use, even when they know that would be better for them. Many will die, unable to resist the urge to use the drug, and many who survive will have incredibly difficult lives as a result, perhaps ending up in prison, mental institutions, or homeless.

It is not clear what differentiates "addicts" from others. There are many theories. People who have gambling addictions have many similar symptoms to those addicted to ingested substances. They have tremendously powerful drives to participate in the activity, it is difficult for them to find reasonable limits or boundaries regarding the activity, and they may risk everything to partake of it. As with other diseases and disorders which relate to the mind, when evaluated by mental health professionals, many of these individuals are found to have underlying disorders of SE.

Is it possible that some people have an SE Switch, which when turned on in the positive mode, have such a flood of wonderfully euphoric feelings, that it becomes virtually impossible for those people not to seek out the activity which is known to produce those feelings? If drinking alcohol not only produces the usual euphoria which most of us have experienced, but for some people a profound sense of being adequate, of being capable or competent or up to the task, perhaps that feeling is what drives the addictive behavior. If picking the right horse, or winning at blackjack creates such intense feelings of adequacy or invincibility, those rewards might be too much for the individual to be rational about. The payoff may be so great for some that only a tremendous, willfully conscious effort to avoid the behavior, almost always in the setting of a group program, could succeed in stopping the addiction.

Probably, if an SE Switch plays any role for this group of people, it may simply be that the reward from the addictive behavior gives them the kind of payoff which would simply bring them back to normal, rather than creating a high which is too seductive to be ignored. In other words, the continuously low levels of SE known to be present in addictive persons, are ameliorated by the effect of alcohol, drugs, or gambling by turning the SE Switch on to the more positive mode. The addicted person would then feel more normal and comfortable during the addictive activity. Rather than seeking a "high," one may simply be trying to feel normal. Betting when one cannot really afford it, gambling when one is deep in debt already from the same activity, may be driven by the quest to feel O.K. about oneself. If one wins, even when overall, the gambling activity produces bottom line loss, the feeling of being capable, successful, up to the task, as good as or better than others, may be more important than almost any other issue for that person who normally does not quite feel that way. The addictive behavior may simply represent the person's drive to be normal.

Chapter 9

Arrogance and Anger

"No man is angry that feels not himself hurt."
Francis Bacon, "Of Anger," *Essays* (1625)

In previous chapters, we have looked at evolutionary psychology, existing notions of SE, the model of the SE Switch, pride, prestige, and "being right," among issues relating to SE. In these discussions, reference has been made to instances where the emotion of anger surfaces in relation to the SE Switch. This chapter deals with anger, experienced when it emerges as a response to arrogant behavior, and how this common occurrence may be related to the SE Switch.

Martina Hingis may be one of the most talented professional female tennis players in the history of the game. Expert commentators, touring tennis pros, and knowledgeable fans agree she has remarkable abilities, making her "game" a pleasure to watch, and a force to be reckoned with by her opponents. At the time of this writing, she is the number one ranked female player on the USTA tour. However, contrary to what usually occurs with great athletes, most fans do not like her and there is reason to believe her competitors do not like her either.

103

Martina is an attractive young lady who has a pleasant smile, but who wears it at times so that it has the appearance of a smirk. Especially when she is prevailing in a match, there is a facial and body language about her which symbolizes a state of mind which goes beyond simple confidence. At these times, she looks cocky and arrogant. In some of her interviews in the press and on TV, she also sounds arrogant, reminding people that she is indeed "number one" and that she knows how talented she is. Other players have become angry with her and the public generally does not like her. Why should this be so?

Why does arrogant behavior make us angry? As already noted, its occurrence rarely impacts on our own life situations in any meaningful way, and yet it feels as if it does. It rarely causes us any measurable harm but we, nevertheless, often react as if it does. Most of the time, when we are aware of arrogant behavior, it angers us at some level. Even when the arrogance is directed at others, or simply resides in the demeanor of a young tennis star, who is not competing against anyone from our home town or family, we react to it with negative feelings. When behavior, in particular circumstances, is present across all cultures, the likelihood is that evolution and genetics have played a significant role in its genesis. We probably feel this way because it has been "selected out," as a trait, to feel that way. Our brain has been hard-wired to react to arrogant behavior.

The model of the SE Switch incorporates the processing of information to tell us how we are doing from moment to moment. As previously described, we receive signals from the limbic lobe telling us, through emotion, whether what is happening to us at any given moment is good or bad, safe or unsafe, worth repeating, or best abandoned. By necessity, this mechanism needs to look at others, in comparison to ourselves, as well as our own capabilities and performance relative to internal standards. We derive a sense of how we stack up against others in various endeavors and also get information about how we have performed a particular task even when there is no direct competition.

We have already touched upon the negative emotions experienced when we are not treated respectfully. As noted, this is believed to be related to the concept of pride and the SE Switch. The extent of our pride is the sum of our experiences of success and failure. It is an account which has credits and debits affecting its level. However, the absolute quantity of pride does not necessarily determine the emotional reaction to perceptions of lack of respect. While there may be a large reserve of pride and self-respect, particular instances of threatening behavior may still stimulate the SE Switch to send unpleasant messages, as was theorized in the Inman case. When an individual behaves in an arrogant manner towards us, the SE Switch receives the information as a threat.

Arrogance is first perceived as a statement of superiority. The "job" of the SE Switch is to protect us. It does so by guiding us with information. If an individual is encountered who is stronger, smarter, more attractive, more capable than we are, it is in our best interest to know that. That is so, because such information helps us to know how to deal with such an individual. Any information our brains can process about another's strengths and weaknesses may be of potential usefulness. Certainly, millions of years ago, in our protohuman states, when survival was foremost in our needs, this kind of information was crucial. Today, it more likely helps serve us in simply knowing how best to behave in particular situations. When we first perceive the greater capability of an individual compared to ourselves, the first reaction we experience is unpleasant. This is the work of the SE Switch. It puts us on notice. When we recognize arrogance in another, we experience, only for a brief moment, the same unpleasant sensation. I believe the SE Switch is the culprit.

Arrogant behavior makes it easier for the SE Switch to do its work. Rather than have to take in many pieces of information to judge the capability of another individual, with arrogance, the job becomes easier. The indicators are no longer subtle or requiring careful cataloguing or sorting for the SE Switch to come to a conclusion and decide on a message. With arrogant behavior, the information "gets in your face." It is easy to detect and process. The individual under surveillance is essentially bragging about his or her talents and strengths. Little analysis is necessary. All the information is up front and available. This is a "no-brainer" for the SE Switch. Arrogance is served up as a fat pitch and the SE Switch knocks it out of the park with ease.

The result is instant negative emotion. It is theorized the first signal sent is that of an unpleasant sensation akin to those present when one feels he does not measure up. This is because the perpetrator of the arrogant behavior is not only tooting his own horn, but incidentally letting us know we are not as good as he is. Implied in the arrogance is the message, "I am better, you are beneath me." The SE Switch first responds as if it is true, warning its owner to be careful. But it also responds to the lack of respect paid by the arrogant individual who assumes he is better. Pride, the bankable reserve of self-respect, is threatened by the arrogance, and the SE Switch takes note, acts and generates anger. The anger is experienced in the same way as if one were insulted.

Arrogance is perceived as a personal insult even when it is not directed as us individually. The SE Switch does not discriminate between whether a behavior is intended to be harmful to us or just looks as if it might. It does not need to make that distinction. It just reacts, producing emotion designed to protect us. Whether the trigger is an overtly rude and aggressive individual who treats us with a lack of respect, or a tennis genius with a smirk, playing in the U.S. Open, we become angry. While our behavior towards the person insulting us is usually different from our behavior towards the tennis star, the feelings are similar.

Arrogance, therefore, causes anger because it is perceived as a threat to our prestige. It is an attack upon our own fitness even though it may be distant from us. Evolution ingeniously provided us with mental equipment to measure both how we are doing and how we are being treated. When we are not the subject of respect we are angered because of the sensations produced within us. The anger may also become a mechanism to let the individual who is not being respectful know that we disapprove of the behavior. It first serves to notify us that there is a discrepancy between our own self-computation of fitness and that appraisal made by another individual, an important survival tool. If then manifested, our anger may also serve as a signal to the offender that we are not pleased with his assessment, possibly also a survival mechanism.

Another kind of anger may be generated by the SE Switch when we do not measure up to our own expectations.

We often become angry with ourselves when we fail at something or think we have. Most of us have experienced this emotion. We talk to ourselves in anger, often with epithets and language we would not tolerate if it came from another. "You stupid son-of-a-bitch." "You idiot." "You piece of crap." We can be as angry at ourselves as with another. Why would we do this?

When we fail at an endeavor, especially one which is relatively short-lived and easy to evaluate, we become angry with ourselves. If we know we need to exert great care not to spill tea while carrying it up stairs, but fail and ruin the carpet, we can become furious with ourselves. Burning the toast, staining our favorite blouse, getting a parking ticket by forgetting to feed the meter, missing an easy shot in tennis, deleting the wrong document from the hard drive, and getting the paint on precisely the object you intended to avoid are mistakes we all make. The anger generated by these failures could also be the work of the SE Switch.

If we have hopes and expectations of success at an endeavor, when we fail, our SE Switches know it and react. They instantly send an unpleasant message to our consciousness. With the purpose of protecting us, the device recognizes we have failed, even if just momentarily, and sends an emotional signal to let us know we need to be careful. Perhaps, "we should not try this activity again" is the lesson, the SE Switch behaving as if our survival depended upon it. We do not like the feeling the SE Switch has produced. After all, if normal, we like ourselves, think we are capable, and worthwhile people. It is as if we have been insulted. When the SE Switch reacts in such a circumstance, it is as though we had been insulted by an outside source, and we react with anger. Since *we* are the source, the ones pushing our own switches into the negative mode, we become angry at ourselves. As previously suggested, we may, in an effort to defuse the unpleasant feelings, also look towards another source and become angry at whoever or whatever is nearby and available. Blaming something other than ourselves feels better for the moment.

In a way, our own arrogance, in believing we are capable and perhaps infallible, may contribute to self-anger. The SE Switch recognizes our own pretentions in the same way it recognizes another's. It is designed to recognize capabilities whether they are our own or someone else's. If we expect to accomplish a task impeccably, our SE Switches may react to our failures with both unpleasant messages and anger. Hubris emanating from self may be seen no differently than when it leaps out at us from Martina Hingis. The SE Switch does not like it. Evolution has imbued us with a response of anger even when it is *we* who are causing the hurt to ourselves.

Chapter 10

Does it Matter?

"Wisdom is the principal thing; therefore get wisdom;
and with all thy getting get understanding."
Bible, Proverbs 4:7

If any of what I have been writing about has merit, does it really pay to understand this concept? Other than the intellectual exercise of thinking about how we feel and behave, and wondering which aspects of those things related to SE may be in some way related to the process of evolution, are there any practical applications? I am not sure, but why stop speculating now.

Evolutionary scientists have been deeply interested in the human neocortex, that largest part of our brain which structurally and functionally seems to separate us from our nearest mammalian and primate relatives. It is this part of the brain which has most to do with our intellectual abilities and our abilities to think, plan, speak, calculate, strategize, speculate, conspire, associate and daydream. This convoluted, complex, outer part of our brain has gotten most of the credit for the great success of Homo Sapiens, our particular species. Compared to other advanced primates, humans continue to thrive and multiply and succeed in even the most unusual and harshest climates and locations on our planet. The process of natural selection, over millions of years, has created this modern wonder of the world, the human brain, which can take in information, think about it, compare it, perhaps talk about it, all at the same time. It can remember, perhaps regret, it can organize, perhaps create, it can teach, perhaps learn, all in the same moment. The brains of animals, who do not have this neocortex, are probably not capable of these kinds of activities. They function more on instinct rather than thought.

If natural selection produced this wonderful machine, the presumption is that such a machine helped the individuals who possessed it to have a better chance at survival. So while today we may use our neocortices to think about what clothing to wear on a given day, our early ancestors used their neocortices to solve complex survival problems, to outwit predators, to deal with the elements, to hunt and to gather. Our ancestors, as well as we, may also have used this machine in helping to deal with competitors for the courtship of members of the opposite sex, enabling the individual to find someone special to mate and have a family with, a very successful method of insuring the survival of offspring. The "programs" the neocortex were capable of "running," including verbal and written language, art, and music, are features of the Homo Sapiens' brain which helped one communicate with another in the most varied and sophisticated ways, leading to behaviors which aided in survival.

If the SE Switch exists, is an ancient evolutionary device which processes information, formulates and utilizes emotional messages as an aid to the individual, what is its relation to this neocortex, a newer, more imaginative and creative part of the brain? Is it possible that this neocortex not only can do all of the things already mentioned, (and these examples are just a small sample of the brain functions usually attributed to the neocortex), but that it can also interact with such an SE Switch? Perhaps the neocortex can help refine and clarify those messages felt in the limbic system, which feel so powerful within us. The ecstacy associated with victory or the agony of defeat may not have to live or die within us just because the limbic system has done its work. This neocortex might help us deal with highs and lows so we are not fooled by either of these "imposters."

Our neocortex helps us to make reasoned, logical choices. By consciously thinking about an issue, we can decide how to deal with events related to interactions with loved ones, friends, coworkers, and enemies. We can be supportive or antagonistic. We can be conciliatory and open, or rigid and narrow in our approaches to people and issues. Our human brains have the capability to make informed, rather than purely instinctual, choices through our neocortex. Because of this particular piece of equipment, the neocortex, we can at least attempt to become the masters of our fates because we have the ability not just to react, but to think something through before acting or making a decision.

Most of us have wished at some time that, when upset, we had waited until we were in a less emotional state before saying something to someone or making some decision. Our emotions often push us to do things our thinking brains wish we had not done. We know at some level that our rational brains should at least participate in the important decisions we need to make. But as previously described, members of our species often behave primarily based upon how they feel, rather than by pure reason. When there is conflict between the two, our intellects often take back seat to our passions.

Charles Darwin avoided public speaking and disliked meetings with his colleagues because he apparently was emotionally uncomfortable in those settings. For a researcher putting forth radical new ideas which needed the support of the scientific community for their validation, his intellect certainly must have told him to get out and mix with his peers, yet he is known to have done otherwise. It would seem fair to say, that in this kind of activity at least, he was governed more by emotion than by his neocortex.

In modern studies relating to national disasters, like hurricanes, tornadoes, earthquakes, and floods, the residents of each of the areas which tend to suffer more of one of the particular types of natural phenomena, minimize the severity of what happens in their own region and exaggerates the severity of what occurs in another region. Since it is highly unlikely that all residents of California inherently prefer earthquakes to hurricanes, it seems more likely that there must be an emotional issue at work instead of a purely reasoned or analytical conclusion driving these "opinions." It is an easy speculation, that the emotion responsible for cancelling out the rational opinion is regional pride, previously discussed in Chapter 6.

Some of the principal persons involved in the planning and execution of the atomic bombing of Hiroshima, with its horrible infliction of human suffering, have defended their actions publicly, unable to grant the possibility that such an act might not have been necessary. If their brains were acting independent of their emotional "need to be right" about such an issue, they would, at least now in retrospect, be able to recognize that an alternative plan might have worked, still protecting our soldiers' lives and sparing the Japanese from such brutality. The point being, not which was the best course, for no one can really ever know that, but whether people who had to bear such a heavy burden of responsibility for making the choice they did were capable of overcoming their emotional need to be right, not to think they had erred, and at least see that there might have been other options. The neocortex and its ability for logic was no match in this instance for the emotional need to avoid having been wrong.

Even with much less at stake in the emotional SE department, in spite of the wonderful capacities of our neocortex to think, reason, or analyze, in situations where choices have to be made, even trivial ones, the emotional side often wins the debate and dictates the action. From the perspectives of respect, pride, "being right," we have already seen how people may be driven to actions which are probably not in their self interest, when they are criticized, insulted, disagreed with, ignored, or treated arrogantly, and become the victims of their own SE Switches. Even with the kind of mental equipment which has the capability of landing spaceships on the moon and finding cures for killer diseases, we humans often allow our emotional reactions to dictate what we do, ignoring the analytical or contextual mind which tells us we probably should behave differently. This phenomenon of course happens with many kinds of emotions, not just those related to SE. When we are upset about something, we may yell at our children, say hurtful things to loved ones, be rude to innocent people, or express anger inappropriately. These are situations where our thinking brain is simply to overcome by our emotional brain. We all have different thresholds, but sooner or later everyone regrets having behaved badly in a situation because emotion got the better of logic.

But back to SE, the SE Switch and the neocortex. So far we have seen examples of the emotional SE Switch derailing the logical neocortex. There is reason to believe the reverse may occur also. Some people seem able to dampen the SE Switch by use of the thinking, planning, analyzing and scheming mind.

If the great 19th century philosopher and psychologist, William James, was right, one's SE is determined by the number of successes one had compared to the number of pretentions or attempts at those successes. The greater the success rate, the higher the SE; the fewer the successes, the lower the SE. Because the human animal is such a wonderful learning machine, this kind of formula would seem to make sense. Our own SE is probably impacted greatly by experienced, triumphs and failures. Our brains have the conscious and unconscious ability to remember and recall how we fared at certain undertakings and I have already speculated that the so-called SE Switch uses this kind of information to make its judgements.

This formula also would allow for high SE by simply having fewer pretensions relative to successes, so it would be possible for an individual to feel relatively comfortable about his SE by simply not worrying so much about attempting to accomplish things. By reducing the denominator (pretentions) compared to the numerator (successes), one's SE could remain in the high range. Is this an example of the neocortex outsmarting the SE Switch? Is this a means to reduce the unpleasant feelings of low SE?

Some writers have expressed the notion that many young people in our society seem to have made a choice not to concern themselves with knowledge, information or accomplishment. T.V. shows like "Beavis and Butthead" demonstrate that you can have fun, be opinionated, and not really have to know much. "Seinfeld," the show about nothing, may have been wildly successful in part because it dealt with the simplest and silliest parts of life and portrayed characters who wrestled with these little challenges, always remaining O.K. Life for them was never very threatening, nor did it need to be experienced at any higher or more sophisticated level for it to be meaningful. The amazingly successful "Dummies" series of computer books implies that it is O.K. not to know very much; in fact, the intention of the books would seem to glorify being a "dummy" and still be able to use a computer.

If there is a trend towards loss of ambition and the drive to achieve in some younger members of our culture, and along with it the need to learn, acquire reliable information and thereby become informed, it may be this trend is producing people who are at least superficially comfortable with their SE. It may just be possible to feel good about one's self, be able to "have a good time" and not be concerned that little is being achieved or accomplished. Jerry Sienfeld, George Costanza, Elaine, and Kramer fit this mold. Is Generation X, at least in part, the product of some need to be happy and contented without having to be knowledgeable?

Our evolution-produced neocortex may have, with this kind of thinking and strategizing, ingeniously devised a methodology to defeat the negative feelings that the SE Switch can produce. By calculating that fewer pretentions in relation to successes produces a higher SE, intellect may have found a way to overcome emotion. No one likes the feeling of low SE, no one likes feeling badly about himself. This modern strategy may just be a more acceptable one for feeling O.K. than other strategies tried in the past. If "dropping out" was in any way related to wanting not to suffer the negative feelings of competing unsuccessfully, that cultural style seems to have failed. For those who have some general problems with their sense of SE, quests for material gain and acquisition of wealth do not seem to make them feel better about themselves even while gaining them some respect, some prestige, and the obvious comforts of the wealth.

We have seen some examples of how the feelings generated from the SE Switch may be so powerful that they overcome the rational, thinking neocortex, and we have also seen how the neocortex may protect some of us at times by confounding the SE Switch, producing comfortable feelings of SE, by logically intending to have fewer pretentions at things. Apart from these examples, there has also been, especially in the field of education, an attempt to instill high SE in children with the belief that, by doing so, the educational process will be more successful.

A SE movement has existed in sociologic and educational fields for awhile. Proponents of this movement believe that low SE is the main thing responsible for many students' academic and social problems. The theory proposes that by supplying plenty of praise and reassurance to students and avoiding harsh criticism, they will develop a sense of high SE which will help them to learn and flourish in our society. This idea banks on the notion that people who feel good about themselves are more likely to succeed, that a confident person is more likely to get the job done.

While this is probably true, namely that someone who believes deep down that he is capable of accomplishing a task has a better chance of success than someone who feels defeated before he starts, the danger is that if teacher's praise and reassurance of his students produces only superficial and situational based kinds of comfort for the students, eventually they will be confronted with situations where an artificial sense of SE just does not work. Simply praising students without providing them with the nuts and bolts skills to acquire and process information and thereby develop the skills to solve problems will eventually lead to situations where they fail and most probably will still suffer those painful emotions related to failure. Albert Shanker, the past president of the American Federation of Teachers, discussed this topic in the last essay he wrote before is death, published in *The New York Times* on Feb. 23, 1997. It seems to me this particular kind of neocortex, strategic thinking, in attempting to harness the forces of SE, does not work very well. Only the actual experience of achievement and accomplishment can convince someone of his ability.

It may be that the most well adjusted, comfortable, successful people in the world are those who have learned how to use the neocortex to deal with the limbic system

116

and my proposed SE Switch. Those people who have the ability to find rewards in the events of each moment no matter what the emotion or hurdle they are facing may have found the secret to blending the multitude of information our brains produce. The ability to become aware of and consciously recognize the emotions one is feeling at any given moment is the first step to being able to use the thinking part of the mind to deal with those emotions in a constructive way.

Rather than simply being controlled by the naked emotions of the SE Switch, negative or positive, and behaving because we feel a certain way, we have the ability, if we can cultivate it, to use our "new brain," our thinking brain, to analyze the emotions being felt, perhaps recognize what has generated them, and behave accordingly. Instead of automatically acting out against someone who has treated us disrespectfully or even arrogantly, if we understood that the rage we felt derived from an ancient survival mechanism within our brains, we might be able fully to experience the emotion, see it for what it is, simply an emotion, and then respond to it in some way which may be better for ourselves and others. This is not to suggest that the emotion is not real, or that it is O.K. for someone to disrespect us but, rather, to understand the nature of our feelings in a situation like this and to capitalize on our knowledge of it, perhaps turning the situation into something positive rather than totally negative. We might even excuse the arrogance of a Martina Hingis, enjoy her tennis skills, and feel sympathy towards her rather than anger, when our thinking brain considers her age, inexperience, and possible parental errors in her upbringing.

When we become angry with ourselves, we may also benefit from a pause, allowing us to use the neocortex, thinking about and analyzing what has just taken place. When self-directed anger develops because the SE Switch has reviewed one of our failures, and reacts as if *we* were behaving arrogantly, we have the chance to defuse the feeling more rapidly and not become victims of the anger. Intellectual appreciation of the circumstances, afforded by the neocortex, permits us to be more in control of what we do than if guided only by emotion. This more recent evolutionary advance in our makeup allows us more opportunity for constructive rather than self-defeating behavior, a potential adverse side effect of the rudimentary SE Switch.

When experiencing the wonderful feelings which emerge from the positive firing of the SE Switch, it would be beneficial not to behave as if we are invincible or arrogant, even if we feel that way. If one could cultivate the ability to enjoy that unique emotion we feel in triumph, but also to have our neocortex looking at, and evaluating what the genesis of such an emotion is, we may be able to capitalize on that knowledge, and behave in ways which are helpful to us and others in the long run. If we can find a way to utilize both the emotional and analytical information at our disposal, then we are making the most of the our highly evolved brains.

These brains have incredible capabilities and potentials. The ability to be aware of what kinds of feelings are generated in our limbic lobes and, as important, why those feelings are generated, may allow us to try other methods to deal with those emotions. Simply reacting to them probably served our ancestors well in terms of making choices and behaving in certain ways. It probably kept them alive.

But we are much more complex creatures. If we simply react, that will not work in our favor at times. When we experience emotions related to what I have called the SE Switch, it will help us understand their nature. Giving in to them, ignoring them, having fewer pretentions to minimize the negative ones, or trying to create positive ones artificially, does not work in the long run. Each of those methods may provide some sense of comfort, but are accomplished at the price of sacrificing other parts of our humanity. Temporary defeat of the SE Switch is not likely to produce long term satisfaction or fulfillment. As with most things in life which are worthwhile, there is no quick fix, no easy path to self contentment. I suspect one must embrace the whole of our brains, be willing to take some risks, and also be able to deal with hurt in order to enjoy the fruits of high SE.

When Monica Lewinsky was asked what allowed her to pursue a relationship with a married man, having already been hurt badly in a prior similar relationship, her answer to Barbara Walters was "my low self-esteem." She believed the negative feelings she had about herself prevented her from pursuing a man where she could be "number one," rather than the other woman. This insight was a touching and probably accurate analysis of one of the factors driving her behavior. But wouldn't it have been infinitely better if Monica was able to have a clearer understanding about SE in the first place? If she had understood what the nature of those awful feelings of low SE might have derived from, perhaps she could have used her neocortex to help her behave differently. Who knows how her life and current events may have been altered if she had?

If medical students, house staff officers, and attending physicians were more aware of the origin of their need to be right, the system of medical education might be improved. The provision of the best medical care, even when one's SE Switch may have fired in the negative mode, could be understood by the neocortex to provide another kind of satisfaction for physicians in training. Lovers, parents, siblings, friends, coworkers, teachers, therapists, diplomats, and politicians might do well to understand how the evolutionary feelings related to "resource holding potential," pride, prestige, and the need to be right, may interfere with their desired goals of getting along. Lawyers might accomplish more for their clients by recognizing what forces may be motivating them. It might be possible for those unfortunate people who have not been able to develop much prestige or self respect to learn to deal with those feelings in more constructive ways. Even those people whose rage due to low SE leads them to violent acts may be able to find better ways of dealing with those feelings. Our educational system might be able to implement more practical methods of instilling durable SE in its students by understanding this evolutionary perspective of its operation.

The neocortex is probably not the only means for working with the limbic lobe and the purported SE Switch. Deep belief in god, devotion to religious practices, meditative techniques, interactions with nature, all seem to provide real mechanisms for some of us to avoid being led astray by emotion. It is beyond my current speculation as to why or how these practices may work, but experts who deal with issues of SE believe these kinds of endeavors have validity and are not simple coverups or bandaids. People have also intuitively, or by direction of their religion, learned that the performance of good deeds seems to help their sense of SE. There is something about behaving kindly or in an altruistic manner towards someone which seems to have a positive impact on feelings of self worth. This kind of activity, as when our neocortex is able to recognize why certain emotions are being felt, appears to be a reliable method of dealing with the negative effects of our SE Switches.

In my own experience, when negative feelings produced by my SE Switch engulf me, I have learned that *recognizing the sensation* is the first step in effectively dealing with the syndrome. Having accomplished this, I try to experience fully the emotion, not trying to minimize it or pretend it is not there. Once engaged in it, I attempt *to think through, as clearly as possible, what factors were present causing my SE Switch to react*. This is not an easy task in the midst of raw emotion, but it can be done.

If successful, the knowledge obtained via the critical thinking is comforting because, as already discussed, we tend to feel better when we can find rational explanations for our symptoms. I then turn my attention *to re-confront the emotion and "be with it" to the greatest extent possible.* Such direct confrontation seems to defuse the negative feelings more quickly than trying to fight them. There is something valuable about focusing non-judgemental attention to an unpleasant sensation. It tends to diminish its impact. People who practice mindfulness meditation know this phenomenon well.

In the case of a negative message from the SE Switch, this method has worked more efficiently for me than for other kinds of emotions. This may be because these messages tend to extinguish more rapidly than others. From a teleologic point of view, this makes sense because the constant surveillance of how we are doing, the SE Switch's function, requires that we process new emotional signals rapidly. Other emotions, like sadness, having little to do with imminent survival, have less need to diminish quickly and so may not respond as readily to direct confrontation.

For those readers who have experienced some of the unpleasant sensations associated with negative messages from the SE Switch, understanding the mechanisms I have described may offer some insight and relief. The method I have personally employed is an essentially risk free venture. While there are no scientific studies to support the method, like chicken soup, it probably cannot hurt.

To answer the question posed in the beginning of this chapter, I believe it does matter. There are good reasons to understand how evolution works, and to know what kinds of equipment we have in our brains as a result of millions of years of evolution. I think it does help to know that what we call SE is a brain mechanism which originally evolved in animals, to help them know how they were doing, in order to help them survive. And I think it does matter for us to realize that many times when we either feel very badly about ourselves or, during those wonderful moments when we feel full of ourselves, that each of those emotions may be the result of the survival machinery which we have inherited from our ancestors. Understanding these phenomena may help us lead richer and more rewarding lives.

Post Script

A surgeon, because he sees exactly what he is working on, always has a good sense of how he is doing at a particular moment. When he finishes an operation he has a pretty good idea of what kind of job he has done. His SE Switch will probably reflect that outcome. Primary care doctors, like me, often do not know how we are doing with patients as we attempt to make our diagnoses and then administer our treatments. We hope we are right and, usually, only time will tell if we were. Our SE Switches are usually in the "waiting for outcome mode" regarding the care we render our patients.

By writing this book, I have become, for the moment, a surgeon. There is no need to speculate and wonder; here it is, a completed operation.

It feels good.

Love that SE Switch.

Bibliography

Alkon, Daniel (1992) *Memory's Voice*. Harper-Collins Publishers.

Branden, Nathaniel (1969) *The Psychology of Self-Esteem*. Bantam Books.

Branden, Nathaniel (1992) *The Power of Self-Esteem*. Health Communications, Inc.

Csikszentmihalyi, Mihaly (1990) *Flow*. Harper Perennial.

Darwin, Charles (1859) *The Origin of Species*.

Dawkins, Richard (1987) *The Blind Watchmaker*. New York: W. W. Norton and Co.

Fetzer, J. H. (1985) *Sociobiology and Epistemology*. D. Reidel Publishing Co.

Fletcher, R. (1957) *Instinct in Man*. New York: International Universities Press.

Friedman, M. D., Alfred and Kaplan, M. D. (1967) *Comprehensive Textbook of Psychiatry*. Baltimore: The Williams and Wilkins Co.

Freud, Sigmund and Brill, A. A. (editor), (1995) *The Basic Writings of Sigmund Freud*. Modern Library.

Gazzaniga, Michael (1992) *Nature's Mind*. Basic Books.

Goleman, Daniel (1995) *Emotional Intelligence*. New York: Bantam Books.

Gould, Stephen (1977) *Ontogeny and Phylogeny*. Cambridge: The Belknap Press.

Johnson, George (1995) *Fire in the Mind*. New York: Alfred A. Knopf.

Jung, Carl and Delaszlo (editor) *The Basic Writings of C. G. Jung.* The Modern Library.

Kabat-Zinn, Jon (1990) *Full Catastrophe Living.* New York: Dell Publishing.

Kabat-Zinn, Jon (1994) *Wherever You Go There You Are.* New York: Hyperion

Laszlo, Ervin (1987) *Evolution, The Grand Synthesis.* Boston: New Science Library.

Lewontin, R. C., Rose, S., Kamin, L., (1984) *Not in our Genes.* New York: Pantheon Books.

Leakey, Richard and Lewin, Roger (1977) *Origins.* New York: E. P. Dutton.

Leakey, Richard (1992) *Origins Reconsidered.* Doubleday.

Maclean, M. D., Paul (1985) *Evolutionary Psychiatry and the Triune Brain.* Psychological Medicine, 15, 219–221.

Maclean, M. D., Paul (1985) *Brain Evolution Relating to Family, Play, and The Separation Call.* Archives of General Psychiatry, 42:405–417.

Mayer, Ernst (1988) *Toward a New Philosophy of Biology.* The Belknap Press.

Masson, Jeffrey (1995) *When Elephants Weep.* New York: Dell Publishing.

McKay, Matthew, and Fanning, Patrick (1987) *Self-Esteem.* New Harbinger Publications.

Mellon, Sydney (1981) *The Evolution of Love.* W. H. Freeman and Co.

Mithen, Steven (1996) *The Philosopy of the Mind.* London: Thomas and Hudson Ltd.

Morris, Desmond (1967) *The Naked Ape.* New York: Dell Publishing.

Mruk, Chris (1995) *Self-esteem: Research, Theory, and Practice.* New York: Springer Publishing Co.

Ridley, Matt (1993) *The Red Queen, Sex and the Evolution of Human Nature.* New York: Penguin Books.

Sagan, Carl (1977) *The Dragons of Eden.* New York: Random House.

Stevens, Anthony (1996) *Evolutionary Psychiatry.* New York: Routledge.

Tiger, Lionel (1987) *The Manufacture of Evil.* Harper and Row.

Unknown author, (1988) *Self-Esteem.* The Lancet, 2 (8617) pp. 943–944.

Young, J. Z. (1988) *Philosophy and the Brain.* New York: Oxford University Press.

Waitley, Denis (1979) *The Philosophy of Winning.* New York: Berkley Books.

Wenegrat M. D., Brant (1984) *Sociobiology and Mental Disorders.* Addison-Wesley Publishing Co.

Wilbur, Ken (1995) *Sex, Ecology, Spirituality.* Shambhala.

Wilson, O. E. (1978) *On Human Nature.* Cambridge: Harvard University Press.

Wilson, O. E. (1980) *Sociobiology: The Abridged Edition.* Cambridge: Harvard University Press.

Wilson, O. E. (1996) *In Search of Nature.* Washington, D.C.: Island Press.

Wilson, O. E. (1984) *Biophilia.* Cambridge. Harvard University Press.

Winson, Jonathan (1985) *Brain and Psyche.* New York: Vintage Books.

Wright, Robert (1994) *The Moral Animal.* New York: Pantheon Books.

Zahn-Waxler, C., Cummings, E., Iannotti, R. (1986) *Altruism and Aggression:* Cambridge University Press.